Praise for *Culturally Proficient Collaboration*

"*Culturally Proficient Collaboration* provides a framework for serious reflection for successful implementation of a comprehensive guidance program."

—Bob Tyra, Project Director
Los Angeles County Office of Education, Downey, CA

"With this book, the authors have bestowed a significant gift. Counselors, school leaders, and teachers now have a clear map to guide our journeys toward equitable service. And all of us receive leadership with this clear application of cultural proficiency, as we work to apply this conceptual model to our specific areas of service."

—John Krownapple, Coordinator for Cultural Proficiency
Howard County Public Schools, Ellicott City, MD

"This is a book that every school counselor, social worker, administrator, and teacher should read and keep on their bookshelves. The authors challenge readers to look within themselves and reflect upon ways they perpetuate and support current counseling practices. The authors leave the reader with a heightened sense of awareness related to Cultural Proficiency Counseling practices and a desire to move beyond traditional methods."

**—Kimberly Johnson-Burkhalter, Equity and
Diversity Educational Consultant**
Wichita Public Schools, KS

"This timely book from Diana Stephens provides the perfect tool set for teachers, counselors, and school leaders. It provides practical strategies for delivering necessary counseling services to the marginalized students who need them the most. An indispensable resource for educators who want to make a difference."

**—Kyunghae Schwartz, Director of
Administrative Support Services**
Ventura Unified School District, CA

"A number of factors contribute to our children feeling disconnected within their families, schools, and communities. This disconnect in our culture can sometimes end in acts of violence by word or deed. Culturally Proficient Collaboration will help administrators, teachers, and counselors maximize their talents and professional training."

—Marie Alviz, Counselor
EP Foster Elementary School, Ventura, CA

"Culturally Proficient Collaboration *is a much-needed contribution to the discussion of our past, current, and future practices in school counseling. This is more than a portrait of the culturally proficient educator—it's a book about change. A must read for anyone in education.*"

—Matthew Meyers, Counselor
Los Angeles Unified School District, CA

"*At a time when many schools do not seem to know what to do with the growing diversity in their populations, this book offers tools for transforming schools into collaborative cultures of care. Stephens and Lindsey are grounded in current best practices promoted by the American School Counselor Association (ASCA) and the Transforming School Counseling Initiative (TSCI), and they recognize the need for school counselors to understand and use data to promote greater equity, genuine cultural appreciation, and vibrant opportunities for all students.*"

—Rolla E. Lewis, Associate Professor
California State University, East Bay, Hayward, CA

"*This powerful book is embedded with meaningingful activities that address systemic inequities within our schools. As we seek to provide the moral framework of cultural proficiency, this book reinforces best practices and encourages us to go deep into our personal interactions with others as educational leaders. Valuing diversity and equity of opportunity goes beyond words in this book and gives us the tools to put our values into action. This book is a powerful reminder of the critical role of school personnel as we hold the privileged space of advocacy for our children.*"

—Trudy T. Arriaga, Superintendent
Ventura Unified School District, Ventura, CA

Culturally Proficient

Proficient

Collaboration

Use and Misuse of School Counselors

Diana L. Stephens
Randall B. Lindsey

Foreword by Trish Hatch

CORWIN
A SAGE Company

CORWIN
A SAGE Company

FOR INFORMATION:

Corwin

A SAGE Company

2455 Teller Road

Thousand Oaks, California 91320

(800) 233-9936

Fax: (800) 417-2466

www.corwin.com

SAGE Ltd.

1 Oliver's Yard

55 City Road

London EC1Y 1SP

United Kingdom

SAGE India Pvt. Ltd.

B 1/I 1 Mohan Cooperative Industrial Area

Mathura Road, New Delhi 110 044

India

SAGE Asia-Pacific Pte. Ltd.

33 Pekin Street #02-01

Far East Square

Singapore 048763

Acquisitions Editor: Dan Alpert
Associate Editor: Megan Bedell
Editorial Assistant: Sarah Bartlett
Production Editor: Amy Schroller
Copy Editor: Amy Rosenstein
Typesetter: C&M Digitals (P) Ltd.
Proofreader: Joyce Li
Indexer: Jean Casalegno
Cover Designer: Scott Van Atta

Printed in the United States of America

Library of Congress Cataloging-in-Publication Data

Stephens, Diana L.

Culturally proficient collaboration : use and misuse of school counselors / Diana L. Stephens, Randall B. Lindsey ; foreword by Trish Hatch.

p. cm.
Includes bibliographical references and index.

ISBN 978-1-4129-8698-4 (pbk.)

1. Educational counseling.
2. Student counselors--Professional relationships.
3. Cross-cultural counseling.
I. Lindsey, Randall B.
II. Title.

LB1027.5.S757 2011
371.4—dc22
2011009924

This book is printed on acid-free paper

11 12 13 14 15 10 9 8 7 6 5 4 3 2 1

Table of Contents

Foreword

The authors of *Culturally Proficient Collaboration* begin by stating, and rightly so, that school counselors are all too often the overlooked educator when it comes to participating in school leadership teams. Although some may argue that this problem exists because administrators don't understand the role of a school counselor, others might rebut that this is because school counselors do not present themselves as competent leaders. Regardless the origin of the issue, this historical concern remains for both school counselors and administrators and must be addressed.

In 1992, Phyllis Hart and Marilyn Jacobi identified six major problems in the preparation of new school counselors and challenged counselors to begin to move from *gatekeeper* to *advocate*. They called for school counseling training institutions to better prepare, challenge and motivate school counselors to advocate for access and equity and to work toward correcting the inequities perpetuated in the educational systems. They suggested counselors use data and become advocates for students with teachers and administrators. Rather than serve as perpetuators of inequity, school counselors could become leaders in systemic change.

Today, in 2011, the National Center for Transforming School Counseling (TSC) posts on its website that school counselors are "all but left out of the education-reform discussion" (The Education Trust, n.d., b, para. 2). It claims school counselors entering the profession are unprepared to effectively serve as advocates for students who need it most—students of poverty and students of color. *There is still much work to be done.*

The American School Counselor Association (ASCA) National Model (2005) calls for school counselors to design, implement, and evaluate school counseling programs. The ASCA Model is the framework for building school counseling programs that includes the foundation, delivery, management, and accountability systems. Within this process, however, are the themes written on the outside of the ASCA Model diamond shape: leadership, advocacy, systemic change, and collaboration. These themes were written to support the school counselor's role as partners in student achievement. I often refer to them as the "blood through the veins" of the school counseling program. School counselors are encouraged to become effective leaders and advocates within schools by collaborating with teachers and administrators to influence systemic changes in school reform.

The ASCA Model also supports the position that school counselors are uniquely positioned to ensure that every student receives access and equity to a rigorous education. The model suggests that school counselors use data to discover inequities, implement plans to close the gap, and then measure the impact. What the ASCA Model does *not* address is the cultural proficiency necessary to become effective school leadership team members. *Culturally Proficient Collaboration* does.

In 2008, ASCA Professional Standard and Competencies were released. Competency I-B-1h states: "demonstrates multicultural, ethical and professional competencies in planning, organizing, implementing and evaluating the comprehensive school counseling program." Again, the ASCA National Model does not address the multicultural competencies. *Culturally Proficient Collaboration* does.

Stephens and Lindsey guide the reader through the historical issues facing the profession and today's evolving new role of the school counselor. This is followed by a description of the *Tools for Cultural Proficiency*. Next they share how these Tools align with ASCA's current professional standards for school counselors. The authors assist the reader, through the use of vignettes, in reflecting on the knowledge, attitudes, and skills they will need to apply the Tools in their work. The vignettes, drawn from real experiences, provide opportunities to illustrate the ideas in practice. Particularly helpful is the *Collaboration Rubric*, which provides excellent examples of cultural proficiency that is informed by either barriers or guiding principles. The continuum of destructiveness to proficiency allows the reader to access her own place on the continuum and, utilizing the *inside-out* approach, begin to access areas of self-growth. Finally, they call for counselors to create personal action plans (much like in the ASCA Model) to address issues of equity in schools.

To effectively partner in student achievement and create change for students, school counselors must possess the knowledge, attitudes, and skills necessary to perform leadership functions in diverse school communities. School counselors must possess the culturally proficient competencies necessary to confidently and competently discuss challenging issues of equity and access. This means learning not only how to analyze data and look for opportunity and achievement gaps, but also gaining the skills to have challenging conversation with professional colleagues about the next steps. *Culturally Proficient Collaboration* provides professional school counselors with competencies to assess themselves when providing systemwide services to all students. The reader is provided assessment tools to increase their own proficiency in designing and implementing data-driven practices. This book serves to provide opportunities for counselors, teachers, and administrators to create more caring cultures within schools.

It is not enough to complain about the policies and procedures that disenfranchise students; it is the school counselors' responsibility to advocate for systemic change and to use their passionate advocacy voice (much like they do for victims of child abuse) to advocate against institutional racism and systems that serve some, not all. Every interaction becomes an opportunity to respond as an agent of change. The work suggested by Stephens and Lindsey addresses this challenge.

The authors are committed to this work. Diana Stephens is a counselor educator who serves as the Chair of the Diversity and Educational Excellence Working Group in the Center for Equality and Justice. She has grant funded partnerships with school districts assisting administrators and school counselors in creating systemic change. Randall Lindsey is a well-known national expert in Cultural Proficiency Education and has written several books on the topic.

School counselors are leaders, advocates, and systemic change agents in our diverse schools. As an integral part of the total educational program for student success, school counselors learn to design, develop, implement, and evaluate their comprehensive school counseling program to ensure that every student receives developmentally appropriate competencies in academic, career, and personal/social development. School counselors are professional student advocates who promote equity and access to a rigorous education for every student and who work to prevent and remove barriers to learning. To accomplish this, school counselor must develop themselves as culturally competent leaders in educational reform and social justice in the schools and communities they serve.

As a graduate student, professional school counselor, administrator, teacher, or counselor educator, I hope you will take this opportunity to reflect on your *inside-out* process for learning about your own culture, the culture of your school, and the culture of the community you serve. Reflect on your thinking and practice, on your intentionality, and your ability to have courageous conversations. Reflect on what your students deserve. In the words of the authors: "get centered, go deeper" . . . because *YOU* are the leaders we are waiting for.

Trish Hatch, PhD
Coauthor, The ASCA National Model
Coauthor, Evidence-Based School Counseling:
Making a Difference With Data-Driven Practices
Associate Professor, San Diego State University

Acknowledgments

We are mindful and are grateful for the many people who have contributed to the completion of this book, the patient support and sacrifices of family, the contributions of professional colleagues, and the inspiration of friends. Our words here are to honor their support for this work.

For me, Diana, it has been an honor and a privilege to collaborate with my coauthor, Randall B. Lindsey, who has opened pathways in my mind and in my practice by his lifelong commitment to equity and access for the children and youth in our schools. I deeply appreciate the reflective conversations with Delores Lindsey, who often touched my heart and inspired my voice as we cocreated this project. I am blessed to have worked with Randy and Delores, dear colleagues, inspiring educators, and special friends. I treasure the place bestowed upon me as a member of the "Lindsey B&B family."

For me, Randy, it has been a soul-enriching and nourishing experience to write with Diana L. Stephens, who continues to dazzle me with her insights about and commitment to the challenges of *living into* a just society. I recall the day I approached Diana and indicated that her experiences and perspective needed to be committed to a book. In our writing together, a friendship has emerged that Delores and I treasure.

A special note of appreciation to Delores B. Lindsey, our critical friend through all stages in the development of this book. Delores asked challenging questions as we conceptualized the book and provided detailed feedback through all stages of our writing. We thank Trish Hatch, for her authorship of our foreword, and for her advocacy in transforming the role of school counselors to better serve the needs of all students.

Our colleagues at Corwin have been, as usual, extremely supportive. Dan Alpert, our acquisitions editor, continues to serve as *friend of the work of equity* and embodies the commitment to social justice we associate with Corwin. Appreciation goes to Megan Bedell, Associate Editor, and Sarah Bartlett, Senior Editorial Assistant, who continue to amaze us with their support, responsiveness, and resourcefulness.

About the Authors

Diana L. Stephens, PhD, is an assistant professor in Counseling & Guidance in the School of Education at California Lutheran University. She serves as the chair of the Diversity and Educational Excellence working group for the Center for Equality and Justice. Her experience as a counselor-educator is preceded by more than 25 years of experience in clinical counseling, administration, and consultation in the nonprofit sector and in private practice. She develops collaborative partnerships with formal and nonformal leaders in schools and communities to increase access to resources for all students in reaching their full potential. She is guided by the belief that embracing diverse perspectives and honoring the cultural heritage of all humankind is essential in achieving personal and organizational success. Diana enjoys relaxation boating with her husband, Steve, derives inspiration from her daughter, Stacie, teaching fifth graders, and finds excitement watching her grandson, Jonathan, play baseball.

Randall B. Lindsey, PhD, is Emeritus Professor, California State University, Los Angeles, and has a practice centered on educational consulting and issues related to equity and access. Prior to higher education faculty roles, Randy served as a junior and senior high school history teacher, a district office administrator for school desegregation, and executive director of a nonprofit corporation. All of Randy's experiences have been in working with diverse populations, and his area of study is the behavior of white people in multicultural settings. It is his belief and experience that too often white people are observers of multicultural issues rather than personally involved with them. He works with colleagues to design and implement programs for and with schools, law enforcement agencies, and community-based organizations to provide access and achievement.

Randy and his wife and frequent coauthor, Delores, are enjoying this phase of life as grandparents, as educators, and in support of just causes that extend the promises of democracy throughout society in authentic ways.

I dedicate this book to my grandson, Jonathan Stephen Karl: May you be inspired in your life journey to fulfill your highest purpose.

—*Diana*

In memory of our coauthor, colleague, and, most importantly, friend R. Chris Westphal, Jr.

—*Randy*

Introduction

Children and youth in P–12 schools depend on educational leaders to guide them in developing positive attitudes, competent skills, and pertinent knowledge in becoming productive citizens. Culturally proficient leadership must be capable of cultivating collaborative cultures of care, inclusion, and respect for diversity in our schools so that our youth can be prepared to navigate within an increasingly diverse, global community. The too-often-overlooked and misused role in school leadership teams is the school counselor and combining their skills and knowledge with administrators and teachers at the school.

Why This Book Is Necessary

Where necessary, schools must intentionally recast school counselors from the misused role of "gatekeeper" to "facilitator." In too many schools the school counselor serves as a "gatekeeper" of the status quo, a role that has maintained disparity in access to resources such as effective teachers, higher academic level courses, and career/college information. Whether counselors have been cast in the role of gatekeeper by their teacher and administrator colleagues or assumed the role volitionally is immaterial. The role of school counselor exists within a context of P–12 education struggling with how best to serve historically underserved students. Schools must make better use of counselors' knowledge and skills by involving them as full-fledged members of school leadership teams. Counselors serving as advocates for all students will be able to assist their teacher and administrator colleagues to focus on broader issues of student access and success. To do so, the school counselor must be a "facilitator," fully involved in school leadership teams.

The 21st century professional school counselor has a primary role in ensuring equitable resources and opportunities for all demographic student groups in schools. National and state counseling standards call for school counselors to identify and provide for the diverse academic, career, personal, and social needs of students (American School Counselor Association, 2003; California Commission for Teacher Credentialing, 2001). Newly trained school counselors are expected to enter the field competently prepared to assess student needs, and to develop, implement, and evaluate systemic school counseling programs that effectively provide resources for all students to be successful. Realistically, however, there are many counselors, administrators, and teachers on school leadership teams in today's schools in need of improved ways of using and improving school counselors' skills.

The Education Trust (1997) established a nation-wide transforming school counseling initiative, calling upon school counselors to be leaders, collaborators, advocates, and agents of change, skilled in identifying and removing barriers that perpetuate the achievement and opportunity gap between more-advantaged and less-advantaged students. In order for school counselors to be competently prepared in meeting these rigorous expectations, they need to team with formal and non-formal leaders in school-based settings that support their skill development. In *Culturally Proficient Collaboration* we guide the reader in acquiring knowledge about requirements for school counselors, assessing their current skill level as culturally proficient leaders, and considering ways of becoming more effective in the multiple roles they assume as school leadership team members.

There is sustained focus on improving the preparation of P–12 school counselors throughout the nation (Ward & House, 1998; Studer, 2006; Wood & Rayle, 2006). Missing from this discourse are the experiences of current school counselors who are facing obstacles and creating solutions as they wrestle with moving from old to new ways of counseling at school sites that vary in their level of systemic support and cultural competency. State and national mandates call for high-quality field experience training for school counseling interns (Council for Accreditation of Counseling and Related Educational Programs, 2001, 2008, 2009; California Commission on Teacher Credentialing, 2001, 2006). Site-supervisors function in pivotal roles in the advancement of the school counseling profession, and in ensuring that all students in P–12 schools receive the support services they need to be successful. The majority of practicing school counselors were trained in outdated curriculum, and they work in collaboration with formal and non-formal school leaders who are often unaware of, or resistive to, the transformed role of the 21st century professional school counselor.

A Practical Guide for Your Use

To ensure that today's school counselors are included in school leadership teams, and are competently prepared to function in our diverse school communities we need to provide rich, reflective resources to guide their knowledge and skill development. *Culturally Proficient Collaboration* is designed to contribute to this process.

A practical guide with strong theoretical framework was the basis in developing this book for teachers, formal and non-formal school leaders to team with emerging and seasoned counselors in developing culturally proficient practices in providing system-wide services to all children and youth. The book applies the *Inside-Out* approach to learning characteristic of the Cultural Proficiency framework to teachers, school leaders, and counselors and to the counseling function in schools. Additionally, the reader is introduced to and guided through a series of reflective exercises that builds knowledge and skill in the core competencies and essential experiences of exemplary counseling practices, aligned with the American School Counseling Association National Model for school counseling programs and The Education Trust transforming school counseling initiative.

The book is structured to support the reader in three significant areas. First, the reader learns about the transforming school counseling initiative, national counseling standards, and expectations of school counselors in support of equitable educational opportunities for historically marginalized populations of students. Second, the reader is guided through a series of assessments that help to increase culturally proficient practices in designing, implementing, and evaluating comprehensive counseling programs that are data-driven. Third, the reader is encouraged to team with school counselors in functioning as educational leaders, advocates, collaborators, and agents of change in creating cultures of care and rigorous academic expectations.

The Education Trust (2003) suggests "Everyone working in school systems has a critical role to play in helping schools meet the needs of underserved students, especially school counselors." *Culturally Proficient Collaboration* provides the knowledge and practices on the systemic role of the 21st century school counselor, to collaborate with all stakeholders in developing effective school environments.

How to Use This Book

We organized this book in three parts to guide and support your journey toward being a member of a culturally proficient school leadership team that values the role of counselor in support of equitable access to educational experiences and outcomes:

- Part I comprises three chapters that provide you with a context for the historical and evolving role of school counselor, a discussion of emergent counseling standards and initiatives, and a description of The Tools of Cultural Proficiency. The fourth chapter brings the new counseling standards and initiative and cultural proficiency together into a rubric for your assessment and planning.
- Part II contains five chapters where you are guided through processes of reflection and dialogue to learn and apply the lens of cultural proficiency to the new counseling performance standards and initiative in support of your students.
- Part III is a single chapter devoted to supporting you and your colleagues developing personal and school action plans addressing equity issues in your school.

PART I

The Changing Role of School Counselor

Schoolwide Leadership

Introduction to Part I

What distinguishes our schools in the early part of the 21st century from their counterparts at the turn of the last century is our commitment to educate all children and youth—from all cultural groups independent of their race, ethnicity, gender, socioeconomic status, sexual orientation, ableness, or faith/spiritual membership or absence thereof. To meet this new mission of schools, the role of school counselor is evolving to include counselors as members of school leadership teams that address issues of equity and access. Chapters 1–4 trace the history of school counseling, describe emergent role and performance standards for school counselors, provide the Tools of Cultural Proficiency as a lens by which to shape the role and function of school counselor, and provide a rubric by which to gauge educator and school progress in effective use of school counselors.

Features of the Chapters

Chapters 1–3 begin with a vignette designed to provide voice to the emerging and changing role of school counselors as members of school leadership teams. The voices are those of educators you will recognize as they seek to improve their craft in service of our diverse student populations. You will be introduced to teachers, administrators, and counselors who represent our experiences with a series of schools and districts with whom we have worked amalgamated into the composite Maple View School District. Throughout the chapters you will learn specific content that relates to the role of school counselors as members of school leadership teams dedicated to improved student learning. At select points in each chapter, you are provided the opportunity to reflect on your reading and on your professional experiences. The final section of each chapter presents a Going Deeper activity designed for you to think more deeply about your role as an educator, what commitments you are willing to make for your own learning, and the manner in which you will work with colleagues for school improvement.

Chapter 4 includes the vignette and Going Deeper format of preceding chapters and adds the use of a rubric. The rubric organizes salient information from Chapters 1–3 in a usable tool. Chapters 5–9 in Part II use the rubric to guide your thinking and plan your actions as an educator and as a member of your school community. Part III, Chapter 10, presents an opportunity for you and your school to develop an action plan.

Glossary

To assist in your reading, we provide you with a glossary of terms. The definitions have been crafted from our more than 40 years of professional and scholarly experiences working with issues related to diversity, equity, access, and inclusion.

Ableism—belief that people served by special education programs and differently abled people do not meet societal standards and are, thereby, marginalized for their differences. This term counters the often-used deficit-laden term *disability*.

Achievement Gap—refers to the disparities of academic success between and among cultural groups of students gauged by standardized or performance-based measures.

ASCA (American School Counseling Association) National School Counseling Model—a framework for school counselors to use in developing, implementing, and evaluating comprehensive, developmentally designed counseling programs, informed by data-driven decision-making.

Classism—belief in the superiority of people in middle and upper socioeconomic classes that fosters a caste system for people in lower socioeconomic classes.

Demographic Groups—alternative to the assessment term *subgroups*; intended to be more specific and descriptive of cultural groups of students.

Ethnocentrism—differs from racism in that it suggests a belief in the superiority of one's own ethnic group, but it says nothing about the group's power to subjugate other groups via societal institutions (adapted from Lindsey, Robins, & Terrell, 2009).

Fellow Educators—our inclusive term that refers to all certified/ credentialed educators serving educative functions in our schools. Using this term, as appropriate, reduces the temptation to ascribe school successes or failures to one educator role—principal, counselor, or teacher.

Formal and Nonformal Leaders—refers to leaders who have been formally appointed to administrative or teacher leader roles as well as emergent leaders generally recognized by colleagues.

Heterosexism—has two components: (a) a belief that heterosexuals are superior to homosexuals; and (b) the power to institutionalize that belief, thereby marginalizing homosexuals overtly and covertly (adapted from Lindsey, Robins, & Terrell, 2009).

Opportunity Gap—underrepresentation of marginalized cultural groups of students in high-level curriculum and course offerings; or, overrepresentation of marginalized cultural groups in special education and alternative education programs.

Racism—has two components: (a) the belief that one racial group is superior to all others; and (b) the power to create an environment where that belief is manifested in the subtle or direct subjugation of the subordinate ethnic groups through a society's institutions (Lindsey, Robins, & Terrell, 2009).

Sexism—has two components: (a) a belief that men are superior to women; and (b) the power to institutionalize that belief, thereby marginalizing women overtly and covertly (adapted from Lindsey, Robins, & Terrell, 2009).

TSCI (Transforming School Counseling Initiative)—a national initiative by The Education Trust to reform the education preparation and professional practice of school counselors as collaborative leaders, advocates, and change agents fostering access, equity, and academic success of all students.

Underserved (or Needing to Be Served Differently)—counter to assessment terms *underperforming* or *low performing* that shifts focus to professional responsibilities of educators and schools.

Underperforming or Low Performing—assessment term used to focus on cultural groups of students performing below a criterion set for standardized or performance-based tests. We offer the counter terms *underserved* or *needing to be served differently* to shift the focus of responsibility to educators and schools.

Resource A, following Chapter 10, provides a storyboard for the vignettes in this book. The storyboard summarizes by essential element the cultural issues presented, The Education Trust's Transforming School Counseling Initiative roles of counselor, the school setting within the Maple View School District, and the issues/action steps under consideration. Brief bios of the educators of Maple View School District appear in the Introduction to Part II.

1

The Evolving Role of School Counselor

How are students different as a result of the school counseling program?

—ASCA (2005)

Getting Centered

Pine Hills High School (PHHS) and the Maple View School District are at the beginning of the second year of its Transforming School Counseling Initiative. Pine Hills' representatives to the district planning team are Emilia, an English teacher; Michael, a counselor; and, Diego, the principal. Join us as they discuss a conversation Emilia overheard among some of her other PHHS colleagues.

Emilia—*Whew! As much as I appreciate our colleagues at this school, I am never prepared for some of the comments made about our students.*

Michael—*Not prepared doesn't mean you're surprised, does it?*

Diego—*What happened, Emilia?*

Emilia—*Well, in preparing for the district meeting next week to kick off year two of the TSCI, you know, that Transforming School Counseling Initiative thing we are doing, I raised the issue of our department and the ways in which we may support or impede student learning and got a lot of push back from two other teachers.*

> **Michael**—*Push back? How do you mean?*
>
> **Emilia**—*One member indicated he took it as an affront that we would even look at "how we impede learning." Another said, "Given where these kids come from, what does the district and their fancy initiatives think we are—magicians?" I might add that he punctuated the word 'initiatives' by using his fingers to illustrate quotation marks.*
>
> **Michael**—*Did others chime in to agree, or did they remain silent?*
>
> **Emilia**—*Good question! Most just rolled their eyes. Let me be clear, I did get some good input. It was just that the negatives always cause me to freeze a bit. I so want to lash back, but I know that usually doesn't help.*
>
> **Diego**—*Which is why we have developed this team approach to the counseling initiative and have taken a multiyear perspective. Often, it does take 3–5 years to change the conversation.*
>
> **Michael**—*I am just surprised they didn't ask, "Isn't it the role of the counselor to make sure 'those kids' are not coddled and to contact their parents rather than depend on us to talk about our 'impediments?"*
>
> **Emilia**—*To be honest, that sentiment was expressed. However, instead of arguing the point, I used the opportunity to describe how the TSCI will support us in addressing achievement gaps. I indicated that the role of counselor is in transition and the new role of school counselor is to be more of a facilitator to work with all teachers and administrators as we continue to face achievement gap hurdles.*
>
> **Diego**—*What was the reaction?*
>
> **Emilia**—*Interestingly, it was mixed. It was at this point that voices began to speak to the progress made last year and that the national focus on accountability seems to be taking a "no excuses" approach.*

How familiar is this conversation to you? Have you heard a similar conversation in your school? Have you participated in this conversation? If so, what did you say? What would you have liked to have said? How do you describe the role of counselor in your school? What would you like the role of counselor to be in your school? Please use the space below to record your responses and related thinking.

Reflection

_____

_____

_____

_____

The Intent of This Chapter

School counselors are too often at the periphery of substantive, collegial conversations with teacher and administrative colleagues about student academic performance. Counselor marginalization within our schools is the result of their being perceived as "firemen" or "therapists" or "schedulers" or any of a litany of roles not central to the core mission of our schools. Unlike teachers and administrators, the counseling profession has had to continually redefine itself in search of a meaningful role in our schools, which leads to the question, *If the role of counselor is continually evolving in a way that is ambiguous, is it any wonder that the role is not embraced by teachers and administrators?* Given the huge task that lies before our schools to educate students from all demographic sectors, we cannot, and must not, let the role of school counselor be at the margin of conversations and decisions about the central purpose of schooling. Counselors must be involved in school decision-making in a way that uses their skills in accessing and interpreting academic and access data. The outcome of such analyses must lead to increased access of students to high-level curricula and result in increasing graduation from high school; students should be prepared to enter colleges and universities or prepared for professional careers.

Our intent in this chapter is to provide you a basis for understanding the changing context for the transition of school counselors from marginalized roles to essential members of leadership teams in schools. The change has not been easy, nor will the transition be easy in the near future for either school counselors or their educator colleagues. In this chapter, you are provided the opportunity to read about the transformational changes that have occurred in the role of the school counselor in service to all students. More importantly, however, you are provided the opportunity to reflect on how you view the role of school counselor in the school(s) with which you work.

Are you ready for this transition in the role of school counselor?

To prepare you for the transition of the role of school counselor, and maybe the very culture of your school related to issues of equity and access, consider the following questions that relate to you. Keep your response to the front of your thinking as you read the chapter.

- If you are a counselor new to the profession, you may be entering a school that is stuck in the old way of doing things and views the counselor as the scheduler who provides mental health support and follows up on grad checks and the like. In what ways might you approach your role as a member of the leadership team?

- If you are an experienced counselor, there are aspects of this changing role that may challenge how you have been doing your job and may make you feel uncomfortable. If you are experiencing discomfort, stay with and understand the feelings. Your reactions may be very similar to how marginalized students feel every day in school and will be a source of dialogue with your teacher and administrator colleagues. Or, this new role may affirm your deeply held assumptions for your role and give you a new path to follow. Be mindful of your feelings of hope and intention.

- If you are an administrator, this change in the role of school counselor to being a member of the school leadership team addressing issues of equity and achievement may mean learning how to work with counselors differently than you may have in the past. What opportunities or challenges might this situation present for you?

- If you are a teacher, like your administrator colleagues, having the counselor be a member of the school leadership team with the expressed intent to advocate for equity and access issues may provide the opportunity and challenge to learn differently. Of what do you want to be mindful about your own learning?

In the sections that follow, you are provided a rich and brief tour through the evolving role of school counselor, from a focus on vocational guidance to mental health provider to the current role of having counselors as lead advocates on issues of equity and access.

Why on Earth Do I Need to Know the History of School Counseling?

An appropriate response to the question posed in the subheading could be, just teach me how to counsel, to provide guidance services, and how to support my teacher colleagues, and I will get the job done. If that would be your response, we would concur but only if we could be assured that all of your colleagues, the principal of your school, let alone the teachers, the assistant principal, and other counselors, all had similar expectations of you and your role at this school. Our experience is that the role of school counselors, particularly in schools that are struggling academically, is often diffused and bears little resemblance to the lofty goals you may have learned in your university preparation program.

You selected this book, most likely, for either of two reasons: (1) you are familiar with Cultural Proficiency and you are curious to see how the Tools of Cultural Proficiency are applied to school counseling; or, (2) you are concerned about the misuse, or underutilization, of school counselors and hope this book will provide direction to make positive impact in your school. For either of these reasons, we believe that understanding how the role of school counselor has evolved and too often kept to the margins of school-based conversations about achievement and access is an important first step in knowing how to embrace the role of school counselor as member of school leadership teams.

This chapter traces the role of school counselor as it has evolved from providing essentially reactive functions of vocational and mental health providers to more comprehensive programs designed to serve the broader academic and social needs of students. As you read those topics, you will note that the evolution of the role of school counselor is aligned with the ever-expanding role of education in this country. The latter part of the chapter is devoted to a summary description of federal and professional standards that support the changing role of school counselor often-unsuspecting gatekeeper of the status quo to the transformational leadership role in schools of today and tomorrow. This emergent, new role of school counselor provides school administrators and nonformal leaders in our schools with a potent team to urgently address and close the too-long-ignored achievement gaps among our demographic groups of students.

As you finish reading this chapter, we believe you will be able to think about and experience your school and school district in new ways. First, you will be able to see with greater clarity the competing views regarding the role of school counselor. Second, you will be able to manage conversations and decision-making that helps guide your school and district to better use school counselors in serving the academic and social needs of all demographic groups of students.

Counselor as Vocational Guidance Is From a Bygone Era

Professional school counselors as members of educational leadership teams are a relatively new concept in the school system, even though school counselors have been part of K–12 schools for more than a century. The school counseling profession, as we know it today, found its origin in the early 1900s in vocational guidance. The United States was in the throes of protest and reform stemming from "negative social conditions" of the Industrial Revolution (Gysbers & Henderson, 2001, p. 246). Traditional farming families were migrating to urban environments and with the social change of this era came public-supported formal education for children of all socioeconomic backgrounds (DeVoss & Andrews, 2006). The necessity of teaching students from divergent backgrounds and preparing them for gainful employment in an industrialized nation led, very appropriately, to the emergence of vocational guidance in schools.

In 1907, Jesse B. Davis, an educator and principal in Michigan, developed the "first systematic school-wide guidance program" (DeVoss & Andrews, 2006, p. 4) when he introduced vocational and moral guidance as a curricula component in an English class one period each week (Schmidt, 2003; Sciarra, 2004). Frank Parsons (1909), often referred to as the "Father of Guidance," was a public school teacher who worked to assist underprivileged youth in seeking employment. Parsons founded the Vocational Bureau of Boston and developed a framework to assist individuals with vocational and career selection (Zunker, 2002). This framework eventually led to the Trait and Factor theory of career development, which links personal traits with job satisfaction. Parsons is credited with laying the foundational work that eventually was adopted by Harvard University as the first college-based counselor education program (Schmidt). Parsons' dedication to vocational choices was instrumental in the rapid development of school guidance (DeVoss & Andrews).

In 1916 the United States formally enacted child labor laws and mandatory elementary education for all children to prevent the misuse of minors as factory workers. The Smith-Hughes Act of 1917 (Stephens, 1995) mandated the continued focus on vocational guidance in public schools, thus solidifying the link between education and counseling guidance. In the 1930s, Edmund Williamson developed the first theory of guidance joining the concepts of individual differences and job analysis (Williamson, 1939). Williamson became a leader in the school-counseling field through his work at the University of Minnesota advocating for the inclusion of student ideas and opinions (Gladdings, 1996).

During the 1920s and 1930s, school guidance and counseling in public K–12 schools was generally carried out by teachers who were appointed as vocational counselors. They functioned in dual roles, maintaining their teaching responsibilities and adding counseling duties. These counselors received no increase in pay and found no formal organizational structure for their new roles in counseling (Gysbers, 2004).

In 1923, Myers expressed concern about the lack of centralized structure and organization of guidance counselors. A growing recognition of the need for "guidance as an integral part of organized education" emerged (p. 139). He sought a centralized unified program and recognition that vocational guidance required specialized training and qualifications (Henderson & Gysbers, 1998). Myers was concerned that the responsibilities of the vocational counselor were misguided and led to diffusion of the counselor role. "Dangerous to the cause of vocational guidance is the tendency to load the vocational counselor with so many duties foreign to the office that little real counseling can be done" (Myers, 1923, p. 141). Some 80 years later, the scholarly literature on school counselors continues to address objection to the myriad non-counseling duties assigned to school counselors.

Who Defines the Role of School Counselor?

An indication of the too- often-marginalized role of school counselor has been that others have defined their role and scope of work in schools. Even a decade after Myers (1923) called for a formalized structure for guidance counseling, the role of the guidance counselor remained ill defined. Without a centralized structure for the guidance and counseling profession, it was left to the principals in individual schools to use counselors as they saw fit. In 1936, Fitch expressed concern about this:

> The dominance of the principal in the field of guidance has also resulted in some cases in an undesirable expansion of the tasks assigned to the counselor . . . there is always danger that the counselor may come to be regarded as a handy man on whom may be unloaded any sort of task that no one else has time to do. Thus we often find counselors performing the function of visiting teacher, director of lunchroom, substitute teacher, counselor of problem pupils, etc. (p. 763)

The concerns expressed by Finch in 1936 continue to be evident in the 21st century in school sites that have not kept abreast of the progress in professional school counseling. As you will see in Chapter 2, the new performance standards set forth by the American School Counselor Association provide a clear indication that the role of school counselor is to be focused around working with teachers and administrators for the academic achievement of all students. It took the latter part of the 20th century for the role of school counselor to evolve slowly from vocational guidance to more comprehensive services.

In 1958, the National Defense Education Act (NDEA) fostered growth in school counseling by funding the adoption of vocational guidance counseling in public schools to identify and support gifted students (those with high skills in math and science). The NDEA's motivation was to keep pace with the growing sophistication of the space program and launching of Sputnik by the Soviet Union. The NDEA also funded colleges and universities in developing school counseling preparation programs (DeVoss & Andrews, 2006). The federal funding associated with the NDEA resulted in the rapid expansion of guidance programs.

Counselor as Mental Health Provider

The mental health profession is intertwined with the school guidance movement. The role of mental health provider is prevalent in many of our schools and viewed as a way to provide services to students not available from teachers. This began in the 1920s when John Dewey emphasized the school's responsibility to promote students' cognitive, personal, social, and moral development. Dewey's position was based on his work in cognitive development. Cognitive development theory suggests that human beings move through hierarchical stages of development. If children are going to learn they must be provided stimulating activities at decisive times when they are predisposed to maximize such learning. Dewey's work contributed to incorporating guidance strategies in curriculum design for counseling programs (Lambie & Williamson, 2004).

By the mid-20th century, "The growth of the mental hygiene movement, social work and child guidance clinics . . . influenced changes in vocational guidance" (Hatch, 2002, p. 11). Although vocational guidance remained a focus of school counseling, it was "overshadowed by a more psychological/clinical emphasis on counseling and by testing" (Gysbers & Henderson, 2001, p. 247).

The work of Carl Rogers and Abraham Maslow changed "the course and direction of the entire guidance movement" shifting the focus from "guidance as vocational to guidance as part of pupil services" (Gysbers & Henderson, 2000, p. 14). Psychologists Rogers and Maslow believed that human beings were born with an inner drive to succeed. Maslow believed self-fulfillment was attainable when a hierarchical set of needs was met. The nonjudgmental, nondirective approach of the humanistic movement became popular "as counselors used this therapeutic style to assist students in resolving personal and educational issues and problems" (Hatch, 2002, p. 14). Rogers' work "changed the function of the training of counselors who were either teachers helping students explore work or counseling psychologists with a psychometric preparation" (i.e., using quantitative tests to measure student intelligence, aptitude or personality traits) (Hatch, p. 15).

In an effort to unify and formalize the school counseling profession, the American School Counseling Association (ASCA) was established in 1958. In the first half of the 20th century of school guidance, confusion had built in understanding just what school counselors were equipped to do on behalf of students. Their role was generally defined and determined by the principal and usually consisted of a number of tasks added to a teacher's other responsibilities. ASCA redefined the profession of school counseling as separate from teaching. By the 1960s, this redefinition led to the hiring of more full-time school counselors to provide guidance and counseling services in schools, thus moving from the prior trend of teachers being assigned counseling duties. An emerging organizational umbrella known as "pupil personnel services" became the structure under which school counselors, school psychologists, social workers, and nurses were brought together (Gysbers, 2001). By the late 1960s, the name of "guidance counselor" changed to "school counselor," as "mental health gained prominence over academic and career planning" (Hatch, 2002, p. 25).

School personnel (i.e., principals, teachers, parents) viewed school counselors as providing services, not programs. The services were generally seen as ancillary or remedial, thus were not considered essential to the educational environment. This contributed to the add-on administrative, clerical duties required of so many school counselors and fostered the focus on the role of the counselor, rather than "the program of counseling and guidance" in public schools (Gysbers & Henderson, 2001, p. 248).

Paradigm Shift

From Reactive Services to Comprehensive Programs

The 1970s brought a paradigm shift by focusing on school counseling as a program rather than myriad reactive services. Slowly and deliberately, the role of school counselor has evolved in a way that is both programmatic, as opposed to offering services, and is expanding to address the educational needs of all students. Like too many change processes in education, the pace of change has been more evolutionary than revolutionary. The good news, however, is the evolutionary developments of the latter part of the 20th century provided a context for the leadership changes needed for today's schools.

A 1977 survey titled *The Status of Guidance and Counseling in Our Nation's Schools* conducted by the American Personnel and Guidance Association (now known as the American Counseling Association) found differences of opinions regarding the "role of the school counselor, confusion regarding the best way to organize and deliver services, and many unresolved issues as to the leadership and supervision of school guidance programs" (Hatch, 2002, p. 32). As a result of dissatisfaction with the direction of school counseling, the emphasis shifted to developing comprehensive programs. Comprehensive programs were designed to support student success in academics, career and college aspirations, and productive citizenship via the development of effective personal and social skills. Comprehensive counseling programming was the framework by which curriculum could be organized and developed in a unified, systematic manner. A number of comprehensive guidance and counseling programs emerged.

Norm Gysbers, a significant contributor to the paradigmatic shift in the school counseling profession, maintained that there was a close relationship between a student's academic development and personal growth (Ellis, 1991). Gysbers devoted himself to seeing that guidance was placed at the heart of the educational process. Gysbers and Moore (1981) drafted *Improving Guidance Programs*, which was embraced by state departments of education and local school districts. Gysbers and colleagues at the University of Missouri-Columbia developed one of the emerging models, the Comprehensive Guidance Program Model, a "student-centered program in the school that is specifically designed to facilitate students' personal, career, and academic development with strong support from and in collaboration with parents, teachers, administrators, and community members" (Gysbers, 2002, p. 147). The purpose of the model is the development of systematic, comprehensive, developmental guidance programs for grades K–12. A core component in Gysbers' model is the fundamental belief that counseling and guidance programs should be provided to all students in K–12 public schools, not just those who are identified as "at risk" or "in greater need" of services.

Johnson and Johnson (1991) developed a model for guidance programs called The New Guidance: Student Competency-based Program. This program also called for comprehensive, developmental programs, but differed from Gysbers' model by focusing on student results, not processes. The evaluation process of this program was different, as counselors were "evaluated on the results of their action, not on how many students received services" (Hatch, 2002, p. 36).

A third model of comprehensive guidance was developed by Myrick (1997). This model focused on counseling, consultation, and coordination as integral to the school's educational mission. "Myrick emphasized programs for all students, an organized, planned and sequential curriculum, and the involvement of all school personnel in an integrated approach" (Hatch, 2002, p. 37).

Standards-Based School Counseling Services and Student Success

Results-based school counseling programs and the federal mandate of No Child Left Behind (NCLB), aligning accountability expectations for administrators, teachers, and school counselors, have emerged in the 21st century. For counselors, results-based programming is not new and has a distinctive history. Analysis of resulted-based counseling reveals that evaluating effective school counseling programs have been evolving for the past 80 years (Gysbers, 2004). Beginning as early as the 1920s, questions arose regarding how to measure the results of guidance counseling. Throughout the 1930s and 1940s, counselor-educators and researchers continued to address the need for more specific accountability. By the 1950s, the focus of evaluating counseling programs shifted from the process of how counseling was conducted to evidence of outcome in how counseling helps our youth in schools.

Gysbers and Moore (1974) described how to develop, implement, and evaluate a comprehensive guidance program. Focus was on process and outcome evaluation. Four questions were asked: "What do we want to accomplish? What kind of delivery system is needed? What did we provide and do? What was the impact?" (Gysbers, 2004, p. 5). These, of course, are the types of questions now driving efforts to close achievement gaps and demonstrate the role of school counselor as resource to school leadership teams. However, because of the budget cuts of the 1980s, school counselors were under intense pressure to demonstrate how their guidance programs made a difference in the

lives of the students they served. Though there was continued discussion in professional journals that accountability in school counseling programs was essential, there continued to be a lack of empirical research being produced. Lee and Workman (1992) noted that "compared to other areas of the profession, school counseling seems to have little empirical evidence to support the claim that it has a significant impact on the development of children and adolescents" (p. 15).

In the 21st century, there is even greater requirement for results-based accountability demonstrating the effectiveness of counseling prevention and intervention programming in contributing to student success (Dahir & Stone, 2003; Hughes & James, 2001; Johnson & Johnson, 2003; Myrick, 2003). The increased focus on accountability is influenced by changes in public education as mandated by the federal government. In 2001, federal legislators passed NCLB, and President George W. Bush signed it in early 2002 in an effort to improve the academic performance of America's children and youth (Yell & Drasgow, 2005). NCLB mandates that every public school in the United States test each student every year and publish the performance results in annual report cards to increase accountability for student achievement, monitor teacher effectiveness, and permit parental choice of schools if their child is in a low-performing school (Yell & Drasgow). The purpose of this increased accountability is "to close academic gaps between economically advantaged students and students who are from different economic, racial, and ethnic backgrounds as well as students with disabilities" (Yell & Drasgow, p. 8). NCLB requires all students in the nation to be proficient in academic achievement by the year 2014. The result of NCLB is that educational leaders in public schools, principals, teachers, and school counselors are being held accountable for student success. NCLB has generated a great deal of controversy in education and resulted in legal challenges by some state departments of education. One of the objections to NCLB is the outcry that standardized testing is not a fair measurement of student ability. Another concern is the expectation that students are to meet one standard of achievement when in fact they receive very different educational opportunities. For example, in higher income neighborhoods, often more resources are available for students. In communities with lower income, the schools are in greater states of disrepair, and schools and communities have limited resources available for students.

The general consensus in the literature is that the expectations of NCLB are ill defined, particularly in expecting accountability by educational leaders when state and federal constituents have not provided the necessary resources to support the needs of educators or students. The expectation that all students will achieve proficiency based on the artificial measurement of standardized tests scores is highly questionable.

However, among the controversy of NCLB, positive considerations do exist. NCLB requires every school in the nation to publicly report test scores for the entire school and to also provide test scores for each subgroup of students in a school. In requiring demographic achievement scores, for the first time in history the public has access to student achievement by socioeconomic status, English-language proficiency and ethnicity. This reporting has revealed the continued and widening opportunity and achievement gaps and places the spotlight on systemic inequities. Students who have continually been denied support for academic achievement are now the focus of educational reform. Accessing this data is essential in creating intervention and prevention counseling programs to promote student achievement. This data can also be used to unveil and to open dialogue about systemic inequities in their schools and in the federal mandate itself.

As the federal government increased accountability expectations in education via NCLB, the school counseling profession has also enacted changes in school counseling programs by developing national standards to guide the profession and mirror the increased accountability by administrators and teachers for student success. In addition, counselor-educator research centers have emerged, showcasing empirical studies that affirm the significant impact school counselors are having on student attendance, academic achievement, and high school graduation rates. Research studies and data on best practices are available through sites such as the Center for School Counselor Outcome Research and Evaluation (www.umass.edu/schoolcounseling/), the Center for Excellence in School Counseling and Leadership (www.cescal .org/), and the Center for Student Support Services (www.sandiego .edu/soles/centers/student_support_systems/san_diego_counseling_ institute.php).

Acknowledging that school counseling is in its first century, we are mindful of the transformation of the profession from myriad reactive tasks to comprehensive, data-based programs and services for all students. The history of school counseling reflects the dedicated work of educators throughout the 20th century who paved the way for the paradigmatic shift in student support services. Chapter 2 brings us into the 21st century with a call to action for counselors and all educators as collaborative partners mutually accountable for the success of all students. As a reader, you will have the opportunity to learn and reflect on the development of national school counseling standards, the emergence of the transforming school counseling initiative, and the paradigm shift of school counselors from *gatekeepers* to *transformers*.

Are you ready for this transition in the role of school counselor?

Yes, we did ask this question earlier in the chapter, and the question is even more relevant now. Neither the achievement gap nor the marginalized role of school counselor can be the elephant in the room that no one can see (or pretends not to see). Therefore, the challenge now before us is to ensure the counselor as a collaborative member of school leadership teams successfully exposing and closing academic and social achievement gaps.

Going Deeper

As you reflect on this chapter, what stands out for you? What thoughts surface for you in thinking about the changing role of the school counselor? As an educator colleague, how do you see yourself, your colleagues, and your school interacting more intentionally with school counselors? In thinking about the opening vignette and the content of this chapter, what did you learn about the evolving role of school counselor? In what ways might this information be useful for you and your school/district? Use the space below to record your thoughts, reflections, and questions that arose.

_____

_____

_____

_____

_____

_____

2

21st Century Counselors Focus on Student Achievement

It is our responsibility, our moral obligation as school counselors, to champion educational equity so each and every student may choose his or her unique version of the American dream.

—Peggy Hines and Stephanie Robinson (2006, p. 33)

Getting Centered

The Pine View Middle School (PVMS) has a student population from mostly affluent homes; however, school personnel have become aware of achievement gap issues and are keenly aware when in district-level conversations that their school has material advantages not possessed by schools on the eastside of the community. For one thing, the team representing PVMS for the Transforming School Counseling Initiative (TSCI) work has identified their school's need to address culture as an asset, not as a deficit. Team members have begun to face the fact that many of their teachers viewed being at PVMS as an escape from their initial eastside school assignments. Pay attention to the conversation among Stacie, the assistant principal; Flora, the school counselor; and, Ed, a classroom teacher.

> **Flora**—*I am looking forward to our year two initiatives with the TSCI.*
>
> **Ed**—*I am, too, and am looking forward to how we can support the achievement gap issues at the district level and anything we can do to support eastside schools.*
>
> **Stacie**—*Of course, we are supposed to focus on district initiatives, but I think our primary level concerns are with this school. We have some internal issues that we are reluctant to face.*
>
> **Flora**—*I agree! I think all schools in the district are intended to benefit, albeit maybe in different ways.*
>
> **Ed**—*Ooops! I think the operative word some politicians use for instances like these, is that I "misspoke." I am very clear that we can learn much on being inclusive of students with regard to race, ethnicity, socioeconomic status, faith, and ableness. I didn't mean to imply that we had nothing to learn.*
>
> **Stacie**—*I know you didn't, Ed, and your recognizing the limitations of your comment so quickly underscore the type of openness we will need to model as we move forward this year.*
>
> **Flora**—*I couldn't agree more! The national conversation so often regards cultural difference as a negative and we know that to be wrong. I am looking forward this year to being with our colleagues as we continue to learn how to build on the assets our students bring to school. I know you, Ed, like most of us at this school view our major role in this school to be learners.*
>
> **Stacie**—*Good point! I attended a national conference and heard the Chief Academic Officer of Wichita routinely introduce her guest speakers as being with them so all can learn together (rather than the presenter being the dispenser of wisdom).*

Pause a moment and think about your colleagues. As you think about the concept of *culture* in your school or school district, is culture regarded as an asset or a deficit? What evidence do you have? Please use the space below to record your thinking—questions, comments, observations, and curiosities.

_____

_____

_____

_____

The Intent of This Chapter

In this chapter we describe changes under way in the role of school counselors. As schools and school districts continue to grapple with the ethical and legal mandates to educate all children and youth to high levels, the role of school counselor is evolving and changing along with the changing roles of school administrators and classroom teachers. Twenty-first century counselors can be at the center of rejuvenated schools as all educators become more narrowly focused on the academic achievement of all students and no longer accepting as fact that *"some kids, from some cultural groups just aren't going to be successful."*

The major topics in this chapter include a discussion of the following:

- The paradigmatic change of school counselor from gatekeeper to being part of schools' leadership teams for transformative change.
- The school counselor's central role in collecting and analyzing with colleagues pertinent data to inform decision-making regarding student achievement.
- The counselor as powerful agent of change for students and the school.

Woven throughout these topics are descriptive tables and narratives to summarize the American School Counselor Association (ASCA) national model and The Education Trust Transforming School Counseling Initiative (TSCI). The ASCA framework provides school counselors, administrators, and teachers with constructive direction on building and improving education programs to serve all students equitably. The Education Trust TSCI builds on the ASCA framework and provides a scope of practice rubric for constructing the dramatic new role of school counselor that represents a shift in counselor role and function. As you proceed with this chapter, you will note the paradigmatic shift in the role of school counselor from traditional gatekeeper to advocate for changes to benefit all students.

At two points in the chapter you are provided the opportunity to record your thoughts, feelings, and questions. Our experience has been that the more you engage personally with the information in the chapter, the deeper your learning will be and the greater positive impact you will have on the lives of students in your school.

Times Are Changing—The New Role of School Counselor

The old counseling paradigm of measuring effective school counseling based on the number of services provided has shifted. The school counseling profession has emerged in the 21st century with a focus on comprehensive counseling programs provided to all students according to their developmental ages and skills. Most importantly, the school counseling movement is aligned with standards-based education, providing greater cohesion among counselors, teachers, and administrators. Today's school counseling programs must be comprehensive (provided to *all* students) developmental (age-appropriate curriculum), and results based (student performance focused to demonstrate effectiveness).

In Chapter 1 we introduced the framework of comprehensive, developmental, results-based school counseling programs developed by Gysbers and Henderson (2000), Johnson and Johnson (1991), and Myrick (1997). The contributions of these notable counselor-educators are foundational to the movement now under way in redefining school counseling. Bowers and Hatch (2003) developed a nationally recognized school-counseling framework known as the ASCA National Model: A Framework for School Counseling Programs (hereinafter referred to as the ASCA National Model). The ASCA National Model is currently receiving exposure at regional, state, and national counseling association conferences, training workshops, and in the curricula of colleges and universities that provide counselor-educator preparation programs. The hallmark of this framework is the data-driven requirement of accountability for school counselors as stakeholders in supporting student achievement. Heretofore, school counselors most often discussed data in terms of the number of programs and services they provided students. Today, school counselors must answer the question first posed in the epigraph to Chapter 1: *"How are students different as a result of the school counseling program"* (ASCA, 2005).

ASCA School Counselor Performance Standards and Competencies

The American School Counselor Association (1998) developed the ASCA School Counselor Performance Standards (hereafter referred to as the ASCA performance standards) to guide administrators (or other supervising personnel) in evaluating school counselor performance in program implementation, evaluation, and professionalism. The ASCA performance standards, portrayed in Table 2.1, contain the

Table 2.1   ASCA National School Counselor Performance Standards

Standard 1: Program Organization:

The professional school counselor plans, organizes, and delivers the school counseling program.

Standard 2: School Guidance Curriculum Delivered to All Students:

The professional school counselor implements the school guidance curriculum through the use of effective instructional skills and careful planning of structured group sessions for all students.

Standard 3: Individual Student Planning:

The professional school counselor implements the individual planning component by guiding individuals and groups of students and their parents or guardians through the development of educational and career goals.

Standard 4: Responsive Services:

The professional school counselor provides responsive services through the effective use of individual and small-group counseling, consultation, and referral skills.

Standard 5: Systems Support:

The professional school counselor provides system support through effective school counseling program management and support for other educational programs.

Standard 6: School Counselor and Administrator Agreement:

The professional school counselor discusses the counseling department management system and the program action plans with the school administrator.

Standard 7: Advisory Council:

The professional school counselor is responsible for establishing and convening an advisory council for the school counseling program.

Standard 8: Use of Data:

The professional school counselor collects and analyzes data to guide program direction and emphasis.

Standard 9: Student Monitoring:

The professional school counselor monitors the students on a regular basis as they progress in school.

Standard 10: Use of Time and Calendar:

The professional school counselor uses time and calendars to implement an efficient program.

Standard 11: Results Evaluation:

The professional school counselor develops a results evaluation for the program.

Standard 12: Program Audit:

The professional school counselor conducts a yearly program audit.

Standard 13: Infusing Themes:

The professional school counselor is a student advocate, leader, collaborator, and a systems change agent.

SOURCE: Adapted from American School Counselor Association (2003).

"basic standards of practice expected from counselors" and reflect the unique training of school counselors and their responsibilities within the system" (ASCA, 2005, p. 62).

The ASCA performance standards can also be used to facilitate school counselor self-evaluation and provide a context for targeting personal and professional development. In addition, the ASCA performance standards provide a framework for administrators and counselors to use in assessing how well school counselors meet these standards. All too often, school counselors are evaluated on a rubric designed for teachers, rather than rubrics specifically created for the roles and responsibilities of school counselors. Administrators and school counselors are encouraged to work collaboratively in utilizing an assessment tool that targets these standards of practices. Table 2.2 provides an abbreviated version of the ASCA performance standards to support the development of an assessment template and to also encourage collaborative efforts in identifying topical areas in school and district development of the appropriate role of 21st century school counselors.

Table 2.2 Abbreviated Version—ASCA School Counselor Performance Standards

Standard 1:	Program organization
Standard 2:	School guidance curriculum delivered to all students
Standard 3:	Individual student planning
Standard 4:	Responsive services
Standard 5:	Systems support
Standard 6:	School counselor and administrator agreement
Standard 7:	Advisory council
Standard 8:	Use of data
Standard 9:	Student monitoring
Standard 10:	Use of time and calendar
Standard 11:	Results evaluation
Standard 12:	Program audit
Standard 13:	Infusing themes

SOURCE: Adapted from American School Counselor Association (2005).

In 2008, ASCA continued its efforts in a unified approach to the preparation and performance of school counselors by developing ASCA School Counselor Competencies. These competencies identify the knowledge, attitudes, and skills necessary to ensure the adequate preparation of 21st century professional school counselors.

The ASCA National Model for School Counseling Programs

The ASCA performance standards and competencies are aligned with the three interdependent and mutually supporting components of the ASCA National Model:

- Collaborative components derived from campus-wide needs assessment.
- Themes of counselor skills and attitudes.
- Domains of student development.

The ASCA National Model provides a framework for schools to use in developing, implementing, and evaluating counseling programs (ASCA, 2003). One major emphasis of the model is campus-wide needs assessments from which the sequence of the four collaborative components are developed and implemented—Foundations, Delivery System, Management System, and Accountability. The second major emphasis of the model is the needs assessment and derived collaborative components to inform development of counselor skills and attitudes in Leadership, Advocacy, and Collaboration and Teaming, and leading ultimately to Systemic Change. The third major emphasis is on providing services for every student on campus in three domains Academic, Career, and Personal-Social Support, often occurring simultaneously to the development of the collaborative components and the related development of counselor skills and attitudes.

Table 2.3 illustrates school counselors as leaders, advocates, collaborators, and agents of change, teaming with all stakeholders in schools and in the community to ensure that every student has access to the support needed for their success.

AUTHOR'S NOTE. The ASCA website provides access to the ASCA School Counselor Performance Appraisal Template, and the ASCA School Counselor Competencies at www .ascanationalmodel.org.

Table 2.3   Logo of the ASCA National Model

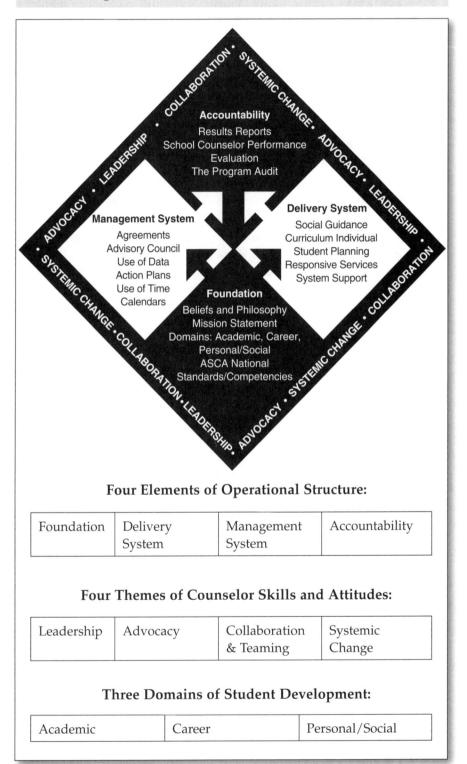

Four Elements of Operational Structure:

Foundation	Delivery System	Management System	Accountability

Four Themes of Counselor Skills and Attitudes:

Leadership	Advocacy	Collaboration & Teaming	Systemic Change

Three Domains of Student Development:

Academic	Career	Personal/Social

Counselors Using Data as a Catalyst for Transformational Change

The early history of the school counseling movement discussed in Chapter 1 described school counselors as ancillary participants in K–12 public schools. Twentieth-century counselors provided individual services such as registering students, scheduling classes, performing disciplinary actions, computing grade-point averages, supervising study hall, overseeing standardized testing procedures, record keeping, filling in for absent teachers, seeing students one at a time for mental health counseling, and assisting with duties in the principal's office. There was no accountability required of counselors to show that students were improving academically. When budget cuts were necessary, the school counselor's position was often eliminated since counselors were not viewed nor utilized as key personnel in supporting student achievement (Campbell & Dahir, 1997).

The 21st century has brought tremendous change in school counseling. Today school counselors are trained as essential stakeholders in the educational process (ASCA, 2005; CCTC, 2001). School counselors are active participants in schools, working in collaboration with principals, teachers, parents, students, and the community in supporting student achievement. They are trained to develop, deliver, manage, and evaluate effective guidance curriculum and counseling programs that serve the needs of every student on campus. Modern counselors are skilled in identifying and creating prevention and intervention programs that support academic success, career opportunities, and personal and social skills for students (Campbell & Dahir, 1997). Counselors collect and evaluate data to ensure programs are helping students. In addition, counselors have a responsibility to identify and rectify inequities in the school system so that all students have equal access to rigorous academic achievement (ASCA, 2003). Table 2.4 describes the contrasting 20th and 21st century school counseling roles.

Data-Driven Decision-Making and Accountability

In the recent past, fellow educators often had the misconceived notion that data-driven analysis is complex and beyond the skill set of practicing school counselors. Teachers and counselors shied away from data collection and analysis in the day-to-day operation of schools. Teachers and counselors alike often viewed data analysis as the sole responsibility of administrators, and, in some schools, administrators held the limited view that data are necessary only for the annual School Accountability Report Card (SARC). School counselors

Table 2.4 From 20th to 21st Century School Counseling Roles

20th Century Model of Counseling:	21st Century Model of Counseling:
Tasks Now Considered Inappropriate to Counseling Program	**Comprehensive, Developmental, Systemic Sequential, Clearly Defined, Accountable**
• Registration and scheduling of all new students • Coordinating or administering cognitive, aptitude, and achievement tests • Signing excuses for students who are tardy or absent • Performing disciplinary actions • Sending students home who are not appropriately dressed • Teaching classes when teachers are absent • Computing grade-point averages • Maintaining student records • Supervising study halls • Clerical record keeping • Assisting with duties in the principal's office • Work with one student at a time in a therapeutic, clinical mode • Preparation of individual education plans, student study teams, and school attendance review boards • Data entry • Informing parents of student misbehavior	• Individual student academic *program planning* • *Interpreting* cognitive, aptitude, and achievement tests • *Counseling* tardy and absent students • *Counseling* students who have disciplinary problems • *Counseling* students as to appropriate school dress • *Collaborating* with teachers to present guidance curriculum lessons • *Analyzing* grade-point averages in relationship to achievement • *Assessing* and interpreting student records • Providing teachers with suggestions for better management of study hall (*consultation*) • Ensuring student records are maintained as per state and federal guidelines (*ethical/legal issues*) • Assisting school principal with *identifying* and *resolving* student issues, needs, and problems • Working with students to provide small and large *group counseling* services • *Advocating* for students at individual education plan meetings, student study teams and school attendance review boards • Disaggregated *data analysis* • Providing parental workshops to support student success (*leadership*) • *70% of time* spent in *direct services* to students • *Indirect services* focus on program *planning*, *maintenance* and *evaluation*, school site planning and *implementation*, *partnerships* and *alliance* with postsecondary institutions, business and community agencies

SOURCE: Adapted from Campbell and Dahir (1997) with permission from the American School Counselor Association.

often lamented, "We just have no time to collect data. Even if we did have time, I don't know the first thing about what data to collect or what to do with it."

The new model of comprehensive school counseling involves the collection, analysis, and evaluation of data. The purpose of school counseling in students' academic accountability is to "show change in student behavior and student learning" (ASCA, 2005, p. 59) and to use data to inform decision-making in ways to increases access to resources for all children.

Reframing Our Thinking About Data

Data are readily accessible; however, analysis of these data requires a shift in thinking about how to prioritize data analysis. Data are used to monitor student process and to identify strategies aimed at narrowing the achievement gap. Twenty-first century school counselors are trained in how to collect and analyze data for the betterment of all educators in the school as well as for the betterment of students and their parents or guardians. Counselors can use disaggregated data to identify groups of students that need additional services (i.e., differentiated instruction, tutoring, support groups); identify barriers in access to rigorous curriculum for every student; create solutions to long-standing truancies; and advocate for adequate resources for students who are systemically underserved because of their ethnicity or socioeconomic status.

Professional development workshops that demystify the data-driven process are available to new and seasoned counselors nationwide. Creating the opportunity for school counselors to attend these workshops is an asset to the entire school. Throughout the nation, school counselors are developing skills in data-focused procedures, and then returning to campus ready to share this information through staff development.

Reflection

What has been your experience with school counselors collecting and analyzing data? What do you think about ensuring school counselors have the time and know what data points to collect at your school site? Consider your position as an administrator, a teacher, or a counselor. What would need to happen for counselors to become collectors of data at your school site? What data would you like school counselors to explore at your school site?

_____

_____

_____

_____

An Illustration of the Benefits of Counselors Collecting and Analyzing Data

So what is the payoff in supporting school counselors in data collection? The following illustrations highlight the contribution of school counselors in using data to increase student academic achievement. A southern California suburban high school counseling team identified the disparity in the Academic Performance Index (API) between different demographic groups of students (i.e., total student, Latino, low socioeconomic, and English learner populations) and used this data to develop and present classroom lessons tailored to the specific needs of each demographic group. In so doing there was an increase in the API scores for each of the demographic groups of students, and faculty attribute the gain to motivational lessons, appropriate course placement, monitoring of student progress, implementation of a tutoring program, and one-on-one conferencing with students, parents, and staff members.

In a southern California urban high school, a new school counselor targeted 30 students who were truant chronically. After gathering data on these truancies, calculating the lost revenue to the school each day by their absence, and gauging the educational disengagement of the students, a strategic plan was put into place. Through meeting with each student, connecting with their parents/guardians via home visits, and establishing resources and services to administer to their unmet needs, 24 of the students were re-engaged in school. The immediate, observable impact was financial for the school (i.e., more dollars each day the students attended); less disruption evident in classrooms when these students were present, which resulted in an opportunity for increased learning (i.e., personal-social issues had been addressed); and a heightened opportunity for academic improvement and putting more of the students on track for graduation (i.e., greater contribution to society at large). More importantly, the school was fulfilling the important moral commitment of taking the initiative to provide for the education of all students at the school.

Data Collection Resources: SPARC and MEASURE

Accountability in school counseling also means sharing successes with others. If we are truly "our brother's keeper," then we demonstrate this by reporting results beyond the school fence. The school counseling profession has simplified the process of accountability by developing templates that are easy to use. Two of the models used in various states throughout the nation that help school counselors report the impact they have on student achievement are the SPARC (Support Personnel Accountability Report Card) and MEASURE (Mission, Elements, Analyze, Stakeholders-Unite, Results, Educate) (www.sparconline.net; Stone & Dahir, 2011).

SPARC is a continuous improvement document, useful in implementing ASCA National Standards, and can be used as a self-evaluation of your student support system: "In keeping with the goal of sharing results with all stakeholders, SPARC is designed to provide school accountability information for a wide range of audiences including: students, parents, teachers, administrators, school board members, accreditation committees, community members, legislative representatives, and other school policy makers" (Uellendahl, Stephens, Buono, & Lewis, 2009). Further information on SPARC is available at www.sparconline.net.

MEASURE is a "process designed to support the goals of the school leadership team and demonstrate(s) that that counselors are helping to drive critical data elements in a positive direction" (Stone & Dahir, 2011, p. 29). Leadership team members will find in Stone and Dahir's third edition of *School Counselor Accountability: A MEASURE of Student Success* (2011) straightforward steps that simplify and guide data-driven approaches.

School Counselors as Powerful Leadership Agents of Change

School counseling during the 20th century paved the way for the new mandate facing school counselors across our nation today—manifesting the resolve, resources, and rigor necessary to bring their voices and expertise to leadership teams on behalf of far too many students who are being underserved in schools. The Education Trust is a leader in this quest, with its 21st Century Transforming School Counseling Initiative. In the early 1990s, The Education Trust, with the support of the DeWitt Wallace-Reader's Digest Fund, embarked upon an initiative to transform how school counselors were trained and used in school settings. Its resolve resulted from the findings of a national assessment of school counselors and counselor-educators, revealing that counselors were not being trained as leaders, advocates, and collaborators. They were most often trained separate from administrators and teachers, with a focus on mental health counseling skills, rather than school-based practices and strategies (The Education Trust, n.d., a).

Subsequent to this national assessment, The Education Trust established the National Center for Transforming School Counseling to provide a forum for including school counselors in the education-reform discussion and to restructure how counselor-education programs train 21st century school counselors. The Education Trust (n.d., b) identified school counselors as "powerful agents of change in schools." It set forth changes in how school counselors are prepared for meeting the diverse needs of students. It calls for changes in university curricular content to address the need for mentoring new school counselors in the profession, and to set forth criteria for establishing collaborative relationships with communities, university/school partnerships, and consultation with state departments of education.

The Education Trust clearly articulates the new identity of school counseling as

> a profession that focuses on the relations and interactions between students and their school environment to reduce the effects of environmental and institutional barriers that impede student academic success. School counselors foster educational equity, access, and academic success in a rigorous curriculum to ensure that all students graduate from highs school ready to succeed in college and careers. (n.d., c, Definition of School Counseling section, para. 3)

Table 2.5 reflects The Education Trust's new vision and scope of practice of 21st century school counselors: Leadership, Advocacy, Teaming & Collaboration, Counseling & Coordination, and Assessment & Use of Data.

The American School Counseling Association and The Education Trust work collaboratively in the transformation of school counseling. Both organizations describe school counselors as leaders, advocates, collaborators, and leverage points for change on behalf of all students. In addition, school counselors are expected to team with formal and nonformal leaders in identifying systemic inequities that

Table 2.5 The TSCI New Vision for School Counselors: Scope of the Work

Leadership	Advocacy	Teaming and Collaboration	Counseling and Coordination	Assessment and Use of Data
Promote, plan, and implement prevention programs; career and college readiness activities; course selection and placement activities; social and personal management activities; and decision-making activities.	Make data available to help the whole school look at student outcomes.	Work with problem-solving teams to ensure responsiveness to equity and cultural diversity issues as well as learning styles.	Hold brief counseling sessions with individual students, groups, and families.	Assess and interpret student needs, recognizing differences in culture, languages, values, and backgrounds.
Provide data on student outcomes, showing achievement gaps, and provide leadership for schools to view data through an equity lens.	Use data to affect change, calling on resources from school and community.	Collaborate with other helping agents (peer helpers, teachers, principals, community agencies, businesses).	Coordinate school and community resources for students, families, and staff to improve student achievement.	Establish and assess measurable goals for student outcomes from counseling programs, activities, interventions, and experiences.
Arrange one-on-one school mentoring to provide students additional support for academic success.	Advocate for student experiences to broaden students' career awareness.	Collaborate with school and community teams to focus on rewards, incentives, and supports for student achievement.	Be a liaison between students and staff, setting high aspirations for all students and developing plans/supports for achieving these aspirations.	Assess barriers that impede learning, inclusion, and academic success for students.
Play a leadership role in defining and carrying out guidance and counseling functions.	Advocate for students' placement and school support for rigorous preparation for all students.	Collaborate with others to develop staff training on team responses to students' academic, social, emotional, and developmental needs.	Coordinate staff training initiatives to address student needs on a schoolwide basis.	Interpret student data for use in whole-school planning for change.

SOURCE: Adapted with permission from The Education Trust (n.d., b).

serve as barriers to student success. The role of the 21st century school counselor is to meet the academic, career, and personal-social needs of all students. This requires meeting with students individually and in group settings. It further calls for the development, implementation, and the evaluation of campuswide prevention and intervention programs.

School counselors cannot achieve these goals in isolation. Accomplishing these goals requires collaboration with others. To effectively identify the needs of students requires knowing who the students are, the communities in which they live, and the family issues they face. Achieving goals focused on student needs also requires an understanding of the organizational culture and school climate as foundational in identifying the systemic supports for and barriers to achievement.

From Gatekeeper to Transformer

In the journey of professional school counselors, the time has come to relinquish the long-held role as gatekeepers of the status quo, and step into their rightful position as transformers of individual and system disparities and inequities in schools. In Table 2.6, The Education Trust clearly defines the gatekeeping role of guidance counselors in the 20th century and the transformation framework for 21st century professional school counselors.

Relationship development is at the heart of the transformational school counseling movement. It is no wonder that school counselors have been identified as key personnel in leading this transformation, as they are trained in relationship building, negotiating differences, resolving conflicts, and setting goals for the betterment of others. University counselor preparation programs throughout the nation are using ASCA's standards and competencies and TSCI's scope of practice to introduce new school counselors to solution-focused perspectives and asset-building frameworks to foster effective consultation and collaboration. Solution-focused perspectives and asset-building frameworks transform theory to practice in the art of relationship development that requires a deep understanding of human beings, a commitment to embracing diversity, and a willingness to remain steadfast in facilitating conversation.

The historical and contemporary creators and facilitators of the ASCA National Model and The Education Trust TSCI have provided a solid framework for the transformation work before us. Adding to this discourse strategies for developing culturally proficient practices will ensure the reflective conversation necessary to advance

Table 2.6   New Vision of School Counseling

Traditional Role – 20th Century	New Role – 21st Century
• Mental health provider • Individual student issues • Clinical focus on deficits • Provider of one-on-one and small groups • Primary focus—personal-social • Ancillary support personnel • Loosely defined responsibilities • Recordkeepers • Sorter, selectors for placement • Isolated work with counselors • Guardians of the status quo • Involvement primarily with students • Little or no accountability • Dependence on system's resources • Postsecondary planners for few	• Academic achievement promoter • Whole-school and system issues • Academic focus on strengths • Leader, planner, program developer • Primary focus—academic success • Integral educational team member • Focused mission and responsibilities • Data users for change agenda • Advocate for inclusion of all • Teaming and collaboration • Agent for change and equity • Involvement with all stakeholders • Accountable for student success • Brokers of school-community resources • Champion for all students

SOURCE: Adapted with permission from The Education Trust (1998).

the effectiveness of formal and nonformal leaders in serving our most precious assets—the children and youth who depend on us for an equitable opportunity to reach their highest potential as citizens and future leaders.

Cultural Proficiency Provides a Context

In Chapter 3, the Tools of Cultural Proficiency are described in a way that provides a context for the role of school counselors that embrace the ASCA domains and TSCI's scope of practice. The achievement gaps that persist in our schools have been documented for 40 years and, thereby, have been ignored for much too long (Perie, Moran, & Lutkus, 2005). The 21st century role of school counselor is one as a catalytic partner with administrators and teachers as we become successful in providing for the academic, career, and personal/social success of students in a context of embracing students' cultures from an assets-based perspective. The Tools of Cultural Proficiency provide guidance on identifying barriers to student achievement and success that reside within us as educators and in our schools, guiding principles that embrace assets within our students' cultures, a continuum of unhealthy to healthy school practices, and standards to guide professional decisions and choices.

Going Deeper

Our first challenge in making the transition from gatekeeper to transformer is reaching an agreement among principals, teachers, and seasoned counselors trained in old paradigms to engage in conversations together in ways that transform our thinking and our practices—one human being at a time, one school at a time. Are you ready for the conversation? Where would you begin? What would you like to say? Please use the space below to record your thinking—responses, comments, or questions that are surfacing for you.

_____

_____

_____

_____

_____

_____

3

The Tools of Cultural Proficiency Provide a Framework for Collaboration

School counselors must be taught to question the beliefs, assumptions, and values behind inequitable school policies, structures, or actions.

—Reese M. House, Patricia J. Martin, and
Colin C. Ward (2002, p. 185)

Getting Centered

Pine Hills High School's (PHHS) Transforming School Counseling Initiative (TSCI) team has immersed itself in learning and understanding the values that underlie the TSCI. Emilia, a teacher at

AUTHOR'S NOTE: For purposes of consistency, material in this chapter is adapted from earlier Cultural Proficiency books, most recently Randall B. Lindsey, Michelle S. Karns, and Keith Myatt, *Culturally Proficient Education: An Assets-Based Approach to Conditions of Poverty*, and Raymond D. Terrell and Randall B. Lindsey, *Culturally Proficient Leadership: The Personal Journey Begins Within*. Both books are published by Corwin.

PHHS, uses Cultural Proficiency in her practice as it dovetails with TSCI and believes this framework would be very beneficial to PHHS by changing the way her colleagues too often view students and community members. As you read the vignette below, be mindful of your reaction to the observations and comments made by Emilia, Michael, and Diego.

Emilia—*This TSCI stuff makes perfect sense to me. In fact, I find it so encouraging the extent to which it aligns with Cultural Proficiency.*

Michael—*How so? Isn't Cultural Proficiency for classroom teachers? Seems that TSCI is geared for counselors.*

Diego—*Uh, let me get in here. I think you both may be correct. Emilia, I have been intrigued ever since you returned from the State Teacher Association Retreat last summer. Your portrayal of the benefits that Cultural Proficiency holds for the entire school intrigued me, but to be honest, I didn't do anymore to learn about it. How do you see it dovetailing with TSCI?*

Emilia—*There are so many concepts that are mutually reinforcing—relationship building, advocacy, and transformational work are all embedded in TSCI and in Cultural Proficiency.*

Michael—*Well, now I am confused! Do I now have to learn about Cultural Proficiency to do the job that TSCI seems to want me to do? Seems like an awful lot to add to my plate!*

Emilia—*To be honest, yes, it does require additional effort on our part. However, what is added is learning other ways of viewing and working with our students and their families. For me, Cultural Proficiency meant unlearning some things so I could learn new ways to work and interact with people culturally different from me. But, in the long run, it doesn't add to the tasks of my job as a teacher; it just supports me as I learn how to do it differently*

Michael—*Hmmm, that is the same thing we are learning about TSCI, so it makes sense.*

Diego—*In some ways, our old ways of operating were much easier. It meant that we didn't have to "learn" or "unlearn" anything.*

Emilia—*You are right, but our students are still failing and underachieving at levels unacceptable to our state department of education and to us!*

Diego—*My point exactly!*

Michael—*I am remembering one of our first district sessions on TSCI where the presenter indicated it takes 3–5 years to "change the conversation" and I am beginning to get clearer on what that meant.*

Diego—*Which is why we are approaching these initiatives in a team format. Though I accept the 3–5 year parameter, I do believe our faculty will find this exciting once we get into it.*

> **Emilia**—*I hope you are right, Diego. Actually, I believe you are. Michael your skills in negotiating differences and resolving conflicts will be valuable in the weeks and months ahead.*
>
> **Diego**—*Those are your skills, too, Emilia, so don't sell yourself short. My role will be to ensure a couple of things. First, that our colleagues have the space to learn skills in analyzing and using data. Second, that we all learn how to engage in conversations using disaggregated data in ways that we don't dodge the difficult questions.*
>
> **Michael**—*You mean, like academic gaps among racial and ethnic groups in our school?*
>
> **Diego**—*Exactly! And, who is overrepresented in special education and underrepresented in gifted classes.*
>
> **Emilia**—*I am so pleased to know that you know, Diego! I was afraid you were oblivious to those gaps.*

Think about the underlying topics of the discussion among Emilia, Michael, and Diego. How do you describe the underlying issues? To what extent are these or similar issues present in your school or district? What thoughts or feelings surfaced for you as you read the vignette? Please use the space below to record your thoughts, feelings, comments, or questions.

_____

_____

_____

_____

This chapter presents the Tools of Cultural Proficiency as a lens for school counselors and fellow educators who want to increase and leverage their effectiveness when working collaboratively in support of students, parents/guardians, and other members of school communities. In this chapter you will find the following:

- The traditional role of school counselor reflects our personal and institutional barriers of school counselors being underutilized in their relationships with teacher and administrator colleagues and overburdened in gatekeeper functions such as sorting and selecting students in ways that perpetuate achievement-gap disparities. Institutional barriers also include the perception of school counselors as ancillary in contributing to student academic achievement, perpetuating a deficit perspective of students as disruptive, disinterested, and defiant, isolating school counselors in cubicles performing one-on-one counseling sessions, and increasing caseloads far beyond the national student-to-counselor ratio recommendations of 250-to-1. The Guiding Principles for Cultural Proficiency are a set of core values to guide school district, schools, and educators to recognize and value the transformative role of counselor to team and collaborate with teacher and administrator colleagues as advocates for effective curricular and instructional programs that focus on equitable academic achievement.

- The Cultural Proficiency Continuum is a tool to identify our unhealthy and healthy values, language, policies, and practices. Table 2.5 depiction of the traditional role of counselors located isolated work, recordkeeping, and involvement primarily with students as functions on the unhealthy side of the continuum. When the role of school counselor is so narrowly proscribed, they too often become guardians of the status quo and, thereby, perpetuate practices that reinforce achievement disparities. In contrast, the emergent role of school counselor as transformer holds the role of counselor to be an agent of change through collaboration and advocacy with other educators in the school/district.

- The Essential Elements of Cultural Competence function as standards by which we develop effective values, behaviors, policies, and practices and, when coupled with The Education Trust standards, provide powerful pathways to serving all students in an equitable manner. The essential elements serve as criteria for judging the reasonableness, soundness, or accuracy of statements, practices or policies. Furthermore, schools, school districts, and educators who hold the essential elements as standards for their collective policies, practices, and behaviors perform as advocates for all students being served in an equitable manner.

Suggested Guidelines as You Consider Cultural Proficiency

As you read this chapter and become familiar with the Tools of Cultural Proficiency, consider these guidelines: Be mindful that Cultural Proficiency is an *inside-out* process of change for individuals and for schools. To support the inside-out process, throughout the book you will be asked to engage in two courses of action, often simultaneously—reflection and dialogue.

- Reflection is the conversations you have with yourself to better understand your values and how they inform your beliefs.
- Dialogue is the conversations you have with others for the purpose of better understanding their values and beliefs. Dialogue is not a debate or a discussion; it is about *understanding*.
- Be intentional in your use of reflection and dialogue, both individually and collectively, to probe and understand the extent to which you and your colleagues believe you have the capacity to educate students from various cultures. This work is not about "all children can learn"; it is about our capacity to educate all children.
- Be thoughtful when considering the guiding principles. People invested in the inherent superiority of their cultures will be challenged by the equitable core values implicit in the Guiding Principles of Cultural Proficiency. This work is about identifying the assets students bring to school and building our capacity to educate.

In summary, the work of Cultural Proficiency is being intentional in our own growth, in the faculty and staff development of our schools as learning communities, and in building on students' assets. A few words about *intentionality* may be in order.

Concept of Intentionality

The guiding principles, when held as core values, inform the essential elements in ways that foster resiliency in we educators, in our schools, and in our students. Resilient educators and schools intentionally engage in professional development to learn continuously about the diverse communities they serve and differentiated ways of teaching, learning, and assessing.

The concept of intentionality prepares you to explore Cultural Proficiency as a set of Tools to serve you as a responsible person in society, as an effective educator, and as a collaborator with other educators. In this chapter we present the Tools of Cultural Proficiency for you to understand yourself as a formal or nonformal leader and your school as an organizational culture in service of students from diverse, heterogeneous communities. In this chapter we introduce Cultural Proficiency as the following:

- A process that begins with us, not with our students or their communities.

- An inside-out shift in thinking for some educators that moves us from viewing students identified as *underperforming* as problematic to viewing them as being *underserved and needing to be served differently* and embracing and esteeming their capacity to learn.
- A lens through which we view our role as educators.
- A set of four interrelated tools to guide our practice.

Cultural Proficiency's Inside-Out Process

Cultural Proficiency is an *inside-out process* of personal and organizational change (Cross, Bazron, Dennis, & Isaacs, 1989). Cultural Proficiency is who we are, more than what we do. Effective use of the Tools of Cultural Proficiency is predicated on your ability and willingness to recognize that change is an inside-out process in which we are students of our assumptions about self, others, and the context in which we work with others. It is our intent to guide you in this book in such a way that you will reflect on your actions, the actions of your school and district, and the cultural communities you serve. This book engages your collaborative leadership journey with activities that have the following in common:

- You will recognize your own assumptions and retain those that facilitate culturally proficient actions and change those that impede such actions.
- You will apply this inside-out process to examine and change as appropriate school policies and practices that either impede or facilitate cultural proficient ends.

The willingness and ability to examine yourself and your school are fundamental to addressing educational gap issues. Cultural Proficiency provides a comprehensive, systemic structure for school leaders to identify, examine, and discuss educational issues in our schools. The four Tools of Cultural Proficiency provide the means to assess and change your values and behaviors and your school's policies and practices in ways that serve our students, schools, communities, and society. Your educational journey using Cultural Proficiency as a means for self-growth begins with mastery of the four Tools of Cultural Proficiency as a philosophical and moral imperative.

Cultural Proficiency: A Paradigm Shift

Cultural Proficiency is a mind-set for how we interact with all people, irrespective of their cultural or demographic memberships. Cultural Proficiency is a worldview that carries explicit values, language, and standards for effective personal interactions and professional practices. Cultural Proficiency is a 24/7 approach to our personal and professional lives. Most importantly, Cultural Proficiency is *not* a set of independent activities or strategies that you learn to use with others—your students, colleagues, or community members.

Too often, we meet and work with educators looking for shortcuts to working with people who live in communities that are culturally different from their own. It is our experience that educators seeking shortcuts to working in cross-cultural settings have an innate belief in their own superiority and view others as needing to be changed. To address such shortcomings, Cross and colleagues (1989) were motivated to develop cultural competence and Cultural Proficiency when they recognized that mental health professionals and institutions often were ineffective in cross-cultural settings.

Educators who commit to culturally proficient practices represent a paradigmatic shift away from the current, dominant group view of regarding *underperforming* groups of students as problematic. Take a few moments and study Table 3.1, the Cultural Proficiency Continuum. Note that the use of the term *tolerance* is associated with Cultural Destructiveness, Cultural Incapacity, and Cultural Blindness while *transformation* is associated with Cultural Precompetence, Cultural Competence, and Cultural Proficiency. In terms of this book, the shift

Table 3.1   The Cultural Proficiency Continuum

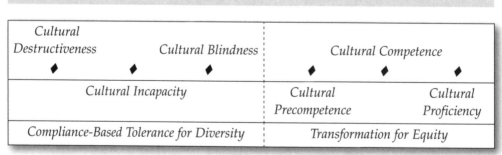

SOURCE: Adapted from Raymond D. Terrell and Randall B. Lindsey. (2009). *Culturally Proficient Leadership: The Personal Journey Begins Within.* Thousand Oaks, CA: Corwin.

from *tolerance* to *transformation* is paradigmatic. In the lives of our students, the monumental shift is from educators holding a value of *tolerating underperforming students* to our holding a *transformational commitment to equity without regard to students' cultural memberships*. The students remain the same; the shift is in our approach to work with our students.

Representative comments from the tolerance paradigm are, *people from that cultural group don't value education; they just need to work harder; it isn't about race or ethnicity, it is about socioeconomic status*; and, *they just need to pull themselves up by their bootstraps, millions of immigrants have succeeded, my ancestors did!*

In contrast, culturally proficient educators hold a *transformational* paradigm that views their work in terms of how they, the educator, affect the educational experiences of people from historically underserved communities. Transformational comments are *what do we need to learn to be effective? What might be instructional approaches that work in this setting? How can our educator groups advocate for equitable distribution of resources to schools in greatest need?* and, *In what ways can I organize the agenda to focus on being solution-centered?*

Cultural Proficiency as a Lens

Culturally proficient educators are effective working with students identified as *underperforming*, the adults in the communities they serve, and the educators and staff members in their schools. Culturally proficient educators are committed to educating all students to high levels through knowing, valuing, and using the students' cultural backgrounds, languages, and learning styles within the selected curricular and instructional contexts. Leaders who are committed to leading our schools in a way that all students have access to the benefits of a democratic system can use the four Tools of Cultural Proficiency as a template for their own personal and professional development.

The Cultural Proficiency Tools

The tables in the pages that follow portray the Tools of Cultural Proficiency as interrelated and interdependent. The Tools of Cultural Proficiency provides you with a moral framework and ethical standards.

A moral framework that juxtaposes:

- *Barriers* to being an effective counselor, against
- *Guiding principles* on which you can build an intentional ethical and professional frame for effective communication and problem-solving to guide your work in service of people in diverse communities.

Ethical standards positioned within:

- *A continuum* of behaviors that enables you to diagnose your own unhealthy and healthy values and behaviors in such a way that you can better influence the policies and practices of our profession, and that presents
- *Essential elements* expressed in terms of standards of personal and professional conduct that serve as a framework for intentionally responding to the academic and social needs of the varied groups in your school and community.

Effective use of these Tools is predicated on a willingness to recognize the assumptions within you and your school. The examination of assumptions begins with you, the educator, not with your colleagues. It is our experience that culturally proficient educators are very clear about themselves relative to working with and leading diverse communities.

Cultural Proficiency is an interrelated set of four Tools that prompt reflection and provide the opportunity to improve your leadership practice in service of others. The Tools provide you with the means to lead your personal life and perform your professional responsibilities in a culturally proficient manner.

The Guiding Principles and the Barriers to Cultural Proficiency

The Guiding Principles of Cultural Proficiency provide a moral response for overcoming the barriers to Cultural Proficiency. There is a recognizable disconnect between the Guiding Principles of Cultural Proficiency and the Barriers to Cultural Proficiency as reflected in educators' *values* and schools' *policies*. Addressing this disconnect is an important step to identifying and clarifying educators' and schools' core values in providing educational opportunities for all socioeconomic groups of students.

Table 3.2 presents the Barriers to Cultural Proficiency in the column to the left and the Guiding Principles to Cultural Proficiency in the column to the right. You will notice a narrow, center column that contains the solitary word *versus*, which denotes the divide between acknowledging the barriers and making a commitment to overcoming the barriers.

Table 3.2   The Guiding Principles and the Barriers to Cultural Proficiency

The Barriers to Cultural Proficiency:	Versus	The Guiding Principles of Cultural Proficiency:
• Resistance to change—viewing change as needing to be done by others, not by one's self • Systems of oppression—acknowledging and recognizing that classism, racism, sexism, ethnocentrism, and other forms of oppression are real experiences • A sense of privilege and entitlement—unawareness or indifference to benefits that accrue solely by one's membership in a social class, gender, racial, or other cultural group		• Culture is a predominant force in people's and school's lives. • People are served in varying degrees by the dominant culture. • People have group identities and individual identities. • Diversity within cultures is vast and significant • Each cultural group has unique cultural needs. • The best of both worlds enhances the capacity of all. • The family, as defined by each culture, is the primary system of support in the education of children. • School systems must recognize that marginalized populations have to be at least bicultural and that this status creates a unique set of issues to which the system must be equipped to respond. • Inherent in cross-cultural interactions are dynamics that must be acknowledged, adjusted to, and accepted.

Reflection

Take a moment and read the words in the first column of Table 3.2. As you read the terms and phrases in the first column, what feelings, reactions, or thoughts occur to you? Please record your responses in the space below.

_____

_____

_____

_____

For many people, the words and phrases will appear scary or irritating. Some readers may respond with feeling blamed, angry, guilty, depressed, or with questions such as "But, where do we go from here?" Other readers may respond by feeling validated, curious, and with questions such as "Yes, so this is my reality and what are we going to do about it?"

This book is dedicated to bringing us together in dialogue with the Guiding Principles of Cultural Proficiency as the common ground for discussion. To have dialogue about the guiding principles begins with recognizing the barriers are real for many people while for others the barriers may be invisible or not recognizable. To enter into dialogue about the barriers and responsibility for addressing them is to be aware of the emotions that exist on both sides of the issue and to be committed to a shared moral commitment of providing equitable educational opportunities to all cultural groups of students in our communities.

As you can see, we present the Guiding Principles of Cultural Proficiency as a counter measure to the barriers and the means to develop a moral frame for recognizing right from wrong and to pursue socially just means in educating all children in our schools to high levels. The barriers represent the intractable issues that have historically, and continue to this day to stymie broad-scale school reform intended to provide adequate and appropriate education to underserved cultural groups of students.

Resistance to change by educators is embodied in two highly observable ways. First, every two years since 1971, the National Association of Educational Progress (NAEP) (Perie, Moran, & Lutkus, 2005) has documented, and circulated widely in the education community, detailed descriptions of academic achievement gaps. Second, in spite of the NAEP data being very public, it has taken state and national education reforms, most widely evident in the federal reauthorization of Elementary and Secondary Education Act (ESEA) Title I's No Child Left Behind Act (2001) and Race to the Top (2009), to set targets for academic achievement in order to hold educators accountable. The continuing presence of educational gaps is a challenge to those of us at all levels in the education community to examine why education and academic achievement gaps continue to persist among demographic groups of students. As a profession, we have acted as if the NAEP data have not existed. We struggle in addressing the inequities so well documented for two generations.

Resistance to changing educational practice is tied to the intractability of systemic oppression such as classism, racism, ethnocentrism, sexism, ableism, and heterosexism. Your response to the reflection activity earlier in this chapter most likely serves as an indicator to levels of discomfort in dealing with these issues. Can you guess how your educator colleagues would respond to the words in the first column of Table 3.2? The dialogue that must take place with and among our colleagues must include discussing barriers to student access and achievement.

The Guiding Principles of Cultural Proficiency provide educators with an inclusive worldview that embraces the maxim that there is no teaching without learning (Freire, 1987, p. 56). The guiding principles are a moral frame to examine the biannual NAEP reports and other data from your school and district and to conclude that current educational practices are not equitable. Accordingly, we recognize that some students are well served by current policies and practices. Unfortunately, recognizing that current practices serves some well often leads to a sense of entitlement and privilege that causes those well served to turn a blind eye to those not well served. It is the dynamic tension between who is well-served and who is underserved that leads us into dialogue and to embrace the moral foundation of the guiding principles of Cultural Proficiency as a framework for serving the educational needs of all our students.

Highly evolved moral development characterizes educators and other persons who hold principled perspectives and who transcend prevailing norms to serve the underserved (CampbellJones, 2002). Evolved senses of justice and fairness lead to using the Guiding Principles of Cultural Proficiency as ethical maxims and the Continuum and Five Essential Elements as behavioral guidelines for educators and school systems alike.

The Guiding Principles of Cultural Proficiency, as represented in Table 3.2, provide guidance for educators' values and behaviors and for the development of schools' policies and practices. Embracing these principles, parents/guardians, and members of underserved communities become foundational to our work and our progress. Adherence to the guiding principles fosters transition to the *healthy* side of the Continuum and the ability to employ use of the Essential Elements of Cultural Competence as standards for personal conduct and school practices.

The Continuum and the Essential Elements

The Cultural Proficiency Continuum and the Five Essential Elements of Cultural Competence provide a template for the *behaviors* of educators and the *practices* of schools. The continuum and elements build on the moral frame of the guiding principles and provide an ethical base from which to make professional choices:

- The continuum describes unhealthy and healthy values and behaviors of educators and policies and practices of schools; in other words, a moral distinction between right and wrong to the left side of the continuum (i.e., destructiveness, incapacity, blindness) and fair and just to the right side of the continuum (i.e., precompetence, competence, proficiency).
- The essential elements provide standards for educators and schools, or, the alignment of ethical principles with educator behaviors and school practices.

Table 3.3 describes the six points of the continuum. Take a moment and read Table 3.3 and note the action words on each side of the continuum. Behaviors and practices located on the left side of the continuum (i.e., destructiveness, incapacity, blindness) give evidence of barriers. Behaviors and practices on the right side of the continuum (i.e., precompetence, competence, proficiency), specifically those regarded as culturally competent and proficient, reflect commitment to the guiding principles as educators' and schools' moral bearing and reliance on the guiding principles as ethical assumptions.

Reflection

Now that you have studied the continuum, what are your thoughts and reactions? Where do you see yourself relative to the students who are struggling academically in your school? Where do you see your school along the continuum? Can you identify practices in your school at each point of the continuum? Please use the space below to record your responses.

_____

_____

_____

_____

Table 3.3   The Cultural Proficiency Continuum—Depicting Unhealthy and Healthy Practices

Cultural Destructiveness ◆ ◆ *Cultural Blindness* ◆		*Cultural Competence* ◆ ◆ ◆	
Cultural Incapacity		*Cultural Precompetence*	*Cultural Proficiency*
Compliance-Based Tolerance for Diversity		*Transformation for Equity*	
• **Cultural Destructiveness** – Seeking to eliminate references to the culture of *others* in all aspects of the school and in relationship with their communities. • **Cultural Incapacity** – Trivializing other cultures and socioeconomic status and seeking to make them appear to be wrong.		• **Cultural Precompetence** – Increasingly aware of what you and the school don't know about working in diverse settings. It is at this key level of development that you and the school can move in positive, constructive direction or you can vacillate, stop and possibly regress.	
• **Cultural Blindness** – Pretending not to see or acknowledge the socioeconomic status and culture of others and choosing to ignore the experiences of such groups within the school and community.		• **Cultural Competence** – Manifesting your personal values and behaviors and the school's policies and practices in a manner that is inclusive with cultures and socioeconomic communities that are new or different from you and the school. • **Cultural Proficiency** – Advocating for lifelong learning for the purpose of being increasingly effective in serving the educational needs of the socioeconomic and cultural groups served by the school. Holding the vision that you and the school are instruments for creating a socially just democracy.	

SOURCE: Adapted from Terrell and Lindsey (2009).

The continuum should make clear the moral vision of educating all students to high levels. Most of us want our educational practice to be on the right side of the continuum and, most likely, don't know how to get there. We may not have the resolve to ask the difficult, courageous questions of *Why are some of our students not achieving?* and *What is in our power to reverse that trend?* "Nothing" is not an acceptable response.

Once the moral resolve of asking the difficult questions of our colleagues and us has been put on the table and the guiding principles are acknowledged as an ethical framework, the Five Essential Elements of Cultural Competence serve as standards for individual educators and schools alike. These five elements become the standards to which we measure the efficacy of our curriculum, the effectiveness of instructional strategies, the relevance of professional development, the utility of systems of assessment and accountability, and the intent of parent and community communications and outreach.

Table 3.4 contains concise descriptions of the Five Essential Elements. Please note the empowering language of learning that is

Table 3.4   The Five Essential Elements of Culturally Proficient Practices

• **Assessing Cultural Knowledge**—Learning about the community you serve, about how educators and the school as a whole react to the community you serve, and what you need to do to be effective in historically underserved communities. Also, leading for learning about the school and its grade levels and departments as cultural entities in responding to the educational needs of the community.
• **Valuing Diversity**—Creating informal and formal decision-making groups inclusive of parents/guardians and community members whose viewpoints and experiences are different from yours and the dominant group at the school, and that will enrich conversations, decision-making, and problem-solving.
• **Managing the Dynamics of Difference**—Modeling problem-solving and conflict-resolution strategies as a natural and normal process within the culture of the schools and the socioeconomic contexts of the communities of your school.
• **Adapting to Diversity**—Learning about socioeconomic and cultural groups different from your own and the ability to use others' experiences and backgrounds in all school settings.
• **Institutionalizing Cultural Knowledge**—Making learning about socioeconomic and cultural groups and their experiences and perspectives as an integral part of the school's professional development.

SOURCE: Adapted from Terrell and Lindsey (2009).

part of each element and that each element serves as a standard for professional behavior and schoolwide practices.

Reflection

In this chapter you have proceeded from a description of the barriers to Cultural Proficiency and have now arrived at a consideration of five standards intended to support you in service of all students in your classrooms and school. How do you react to the essential elements? In what way do the essential elements reflect the ethics in the Guiding Principles of Cultural Proficiency? To what extent do you want these standards to serve your educational practice and that of your school in service of historically underserved students? Please use the space below to record your responses.

_____

_____

_____

_____

Please note that the Five Essential Elements exist at the *cultural competence* point of the continuum. Proficiency is when an educator or school has incorporated the essential elements into their practice to the extent that they develop at least these commitments:

- A commitment to one's own learning as an on-going immutable process.
- A commitment to social justice that addresses the educational needs of all current and emerging cultural groups in the school and community.
- A commitment to advocacy that is natural, normal, and effective.
- A commitment to mentoring the underserved to have access to educational opportunity and to mentoring those well served by current practice to become aware of and responsive to underserved individuals and cultural groups. The underserved could be colleagues, students, or members of the community from cultural groups marginalized and not included in discussion and decision-making groups that would benefit from their expertise and perspectives.

Schools as middle-class entities can well serve diverse and often low-income and impoverished communities when we educators view our role as providing the knowledge and skills for community members to pursue their own self-interests. In doing so, students are viewed as competent and worthy of a high-quality educational experience.

Cultural Proficiency and Counselors

Twenty-first century school counselors serve as leaders who advocate for the needs and services of all students in K–12 schools, and identify systemic inequities that hinder access to resources for students who are underserved. The moral imperative to ensure equitable opportunity for all students requires a resolve and ability to engage in artful communication with fellow educators, parents/guardians, staff, and community partners from diverse backgrounds. Though counselors are skilled in effective communication skills, their experience in initiating, leading, and sustaining dialogue with others is far too often hindered by limited knowledge and expertise in ways to encourage, facilitate, and embrace diverse perspectives. Far beyond their own life experience and professional training, school counselors will find themselves interacting with a variety of cultures. Navigating beliefs and practices unfamiliar to them requires ongoing self-reflection to identify their own values and perspectives and to honor the perspectives of others that may vastly differ from their own. This is not an easy task, as our heritage, beliefs, and value systems are dear to each of us, and thus can evoke intense emotion within self and others when questioned or examined.

The Cultural Proficiency Counselor Collaboration Rubric presented in Chapter 4 provides specific language and tools for counselors and fellow educators who are in the unique position of bridging communication and ideological gaps that are imbedded in systems of oppression for some and entitlement for others. Counselors may find themselves pressured to disregard policies and practices that perpetuate inequity and injustice in schools, and to avoid conversations around issues of race, gender, sexual orientation, faith, class, and ableness. Identifying the barriers and understanding the Guiding Principles of Cultural Proficiency can help counselors mitigate the human tendency to avoid or minimize that which makes them or others uncomfortable or challenges their beliefs. The essential elements will aid the school counselor in teaming and leading with others in the creation of institutional policies and practices that ensure every student equal access to resources. The continuum helps counselors identify unhealthy practices that hinder student achievement in schools and to facilitate and engage in healthy dialogue aimed at transforming the school culture and organizational climate in ways that honor the richness of diversity and prepares every student for academic success and good citizenship.

Going Deeper

What have you learned in this chapter? What new questions do you now have? Thinking of your role as an educator, how does the information from this chapter cause you to think differently about your practice? How does this information cause you to think differently about your school/district? How does this chapter cause you to think differently about students too often described as *underperforming*?

_____

_____

_____

_____

_____

_____

_____

_____

4

Counselor Collaboration Rubric: Misuse to Use

We need to stop asking ourselves about the meaning of life. . . . Life ultimately means taking the responsibility to find the right answer to its problems and to fulfill the tasks which it constantly sets for each individual.

—Viktor Frankl (1984, p. 98)

Getting Centered

Closing achievement gaps emerged as a hot topic issue in the first decade of the 21st century throughout the country. Take a moment and think about how you and your school address issues of equity and access. How do you describe the typical roles of teachers, administrators, and counselors in those discussions? Who takes the lead in posing questions? Who brings data to the discussions? How do people react to data that portray disparities among demographic/ cultural groups of students? What would you like to know or be able to do to support quality collegial conversations? Please use the space below to record your thinking.

_____

_____

_____

_____

The preceding chapters discussed how important the school counselor could be to school leadership teams for transforming school practices to ensure all cultural/demographic groups of students have access to high-quality education. This chapter introduces you to a rubric that aligns the American School Counselor Association's (ASCA) domains and the Transforming School Counseling Initiative's (TSCI) scope and practice with the Tools of Cultural Proficiency. The rubric brings these three important resources as partners in service of school counselor roles with school leadership teams to use as a leverage point for change:

- The ASCA academic, career, and personal/social success domains.
- TSCI's 21st century role of school counselor.
- The Tools of Cultural Proficiency.

Table 4.1 presents the Counselor Collaboration Rubric: Misuse to Use. The descriptions under the first column are operational descriptions of the role of school counselor for each essential element. The guide in how to read the rubric follows the rubric.

Please use this guide for reading and interpreting Table 4.1, the Counselor Collaboration Rubric: Misuse to Use.

- Note the rubric comprises rows and columns.
- Each of the rows is one of the five standards referred to as an *Essential Element of Cultural Competence*.
- There are seven columns. At the top of the first column is the title *Essential Elements*. A brief description of the element is given in the context of the topic and the role of school counselor.
- Each of the next six columns is one of the six points of the *Cultural Proficiency* Continuum.
- The sixth column is titled *Cultural Competence*. Each of the descriptors in that column describes one of the essential elements of cultural competence. The language is in active voice and describes actions that can be taken today in schools. It is at Cultural Competence that a standard is deemed to have been "met."

- The seventh column is titled *Cultural Proficiency*. The description is future focused and measurable.

Unpacking the Rubric

Once you have become familiar with the rubric, following are a couple of activities you can use to deepen your understanding of the rubric and the role of counselor as a leverage point for change. These activities are also highly effective professional development activities you can use with colleagues.

Adjectives and Verbs

The first activity is to analyze the rubric to understand and be able to use the rubric as a diagnostic and planning tool. Follow these steps:

1. Turn your attention to the first essential element, Assessing Cultural Knowledge.

2. Study the operational definition of Assessing Cultural Knowledge in the first column. We refer to this definition as the *essence* of the essential element.

3. Next, read the examples for Assessing Cultural Knowledge, beginning with Cultural Destructiveness and through Cultural Proficiency. You will have read six illustrations along the Continuum.

4. Now, go back through the six illustrations and circle or highlight verbs and adjectives. What do you notice as you read from left to right? Record your observations and reactions.

5. If conducting the activity with colleagues, compare and discuss your observations and reactions.

6. Finally, perform the same analysis with the remaining four essential elements—Valuing Diversity, Managing the Dynamics of Difference, Adapting to Diversity, and Institutionalizing Cultural Knowledge.

Upon completing this activity, you will be equipped to use the rubric to diagnose your values and behaviors and your school's policies and practices. In the section, Uses of the Rubric, we describe diagnostic applications of the rubric.

Table 4.1   Counselor Collaboration Rubric: Misuse to Use

Operational Definition of Essential Elements	Informed by Barriers to Cultural Proficiency		
	Cultural Destructiveness	Cultural Incapacity	Cultural Blindness
Assessing Cultural Knowledge—extent to which counselors initiate learning about their own and others' culture(s) as assets and about the school as a cultural entity.	School culture supports counselor's role to remove unruly students from classroom to protect learning environment of other students. Counselor's role is to transform the student to be a nondisruptive member of the classroom.	School culture defines role of counselor as scheduler, tardy sweeps, lunch duty, and "running groups" and the counselor accedes to it. The counselor fails to respond when knowing this is not appropriate. Counselors and fellow educators don't recognize when student's experience is being infringed upon and responds in an interrogative, accusing, blaming manner and refers to student behavior as "what can you expect from *students like these*." Student behaviors are interpreted as defiant and disrespectful.	Counselors acquiesce to leadership team adopting programs for student personal/social success that focuses on control and compliance and ignores relationship of culture (student, staff, school) to learning.

Stephens, Diana L., & Lindsey, Randall B. (2011). *Culturally proficient collaboration: Use and misuse of sch*

Informed by Guiding Principles of Cultural Proficiency		
Cultural Precompetence	**Cultural Competence— Informed by TSCI**	**Cultural Proficiency**
Counselors and fellow educators acknowledge gaps in own and colleagues' knowledge about student and community cultures as assets and assume initiative to inform leadership team of need for self-study.	Counselors' role on leadership teams includes using the lens of educators' and students' personal culture and the schools' organizational culture as assets in providing responsive educational programs. *Counselor role is:* • Leader, planner, program developer • Involved with all stakeholders • To maintain academic focus on strengths	Counselor role viewed as catalytic advocate for social justice and lifelong learning for school personnel. Academic, career, and personal/social success of all students is primary and interdependent focus.

(Continued)

Table 4.1 (Continued)

Operational Definition of Essential Elements	Informed by Barriers to Cultural Proficiency		
	Cultural Destructiveness	Cultural Incapacity	Cultural Blindness
Valuing Diversity—extent to which informal and formal decision-making groups are inclusive of people whose viewpoints and experiences are different from the counselor and the dominant group at the school.	Counselors and fellow educators schedule parent/guardian contact at the convenience of the school and regard parent/guardian nonattendance as evidence of non-interest in their children's education.	Counselors and fellow educators express a sense of pity toward students found not meeting school expectations and mistakenly judge students' home situations as a cultural liability and reason for parent or guardian non-responsiveness. Students are further isolated and less able to interact effectively outside the classrooms.	Counselors and fellow educators grudgingly comply with legal requirements for advisory groups and regard such requirements as window dressing. Counselors feel confident in how to confront issues of student aggressiveness but not how to recognize when aggressiveness is caused by hostile school climate.

Stephens, Diana L., & Lindsey, Randall B. (2011). *Culturally proficient collaboration: Use and misuse of sch*

Informed by Guiding Principles of Cultural Proficiency		
Cultural Precompetence	**Cultural Competence— Informed by TSCI**	**Cultural Proficiency**
Counselors and fellow educators become aware that colleagues have limited knowledge about student cultures or the impact of negative school climate. Counselors are not sure how to access informal and formal decision-making groups within the school or community for information or support. Similarly, they don't know how to present such information to colleagues.	Counselors work with other educators to analyze disaggregated data on achievement and climate issues as a means to identify school strengths and to lay plans for addressing disparities. Counselors and educator colleagues meet regularly with constituent groups to examine data for purpose of identifying multiple interpretations of data that may inform prevalent policy and practice that considers access and inclusion as means to closing achievement gaps. *Counselor role is:* <ul><li>Agent for change & equity.</li><li>Champion for all students.</li><li>Advocate for inclusion of all.</li></ul>	Counselors work with other educators to develop and conduct a professional development plan that involves parents/ guardians and key community people to examine achievement data and data that illustrates suspensions, expulsions, assignment in special needs and gifted programs by demographic groups to make known disparities as focus for on-going professional development.

(Continued)

Table 4.1 (Continued)

Operational Definition of Essential Elements	Informed by Barriers to Cultural Proficiency		
	Cultural Destructiveness	Cultural Incapacity	Cultural Blindnes‹
Managing the Dynamics of Difference—the extent to which counselors use problem-solving and conflict strategies as ways to be inclusive of multiple perspectives.	Counselors and fellow educators implement zero tolerance policies that impose punishment and view situations as resolved. Providing no support for returning students after punishment (i.e., suspension) to learn improved ways of dealing with situations at school—and yet expecting students to have "changed" by the punishment. This assumes that students know what to do, and are just selecting to defy and disregard rules.	Counselors are expected to perform effectively in conflict situations without considering underlying dynamics of cultural conflict. Counselors and fellow educators often resist counselors being included in everyday situations of students' academic pursuits.	Counselors and fellow educators don't see a need to understand cultural nuances believing that counseling skills and relationship building is the same irrespective of cultural background.

Stephens, Diana L., & Lindsey, Randall B. (2011). *Culturally proficient collaboration: Use and misuse of sch‹*

	Informed by Guiding Principles of Cultural Proficiency	
Cultural Precompetence	**Cultural Competence— Informed by TSCI**	**Cultural Proficiency**
Counselors and fellow educators begin to collaborate in developing within academic curricular content personal-social areas that increase potential for lifelong success of students.	Counselors and educator colleagues conduct data examination sessions within the school and with constituents to foster discussions that surface divergent perspectives in a manner that addresses demographic groups of students who have been marginalized within the school culture. *Counselor role is:* <ul><li>Broker of school-community resources.</li><li>Data user for change agenda.</li><li>To be accountable for student success.</li></ul>	Counselors work with other educators and community members to address equity issue disparities at all levels of governance—local, district, state, and with educators' professional organizations.

(Continued)

Table 4.1 (Continued)

Operational Definition of Essential Elements	Informed by Barriers to Cultural Proficiency		
	Cultural Destructiveness	Cultural Incapacity	Cultural Blindness
Adapting to Diversity—extent to which cultural knowledge is integrated into the values of the counselor and fellow educators and into the policies of the school.	Counselors and fellow educators adhere to the belief that recognizing culture is a distraction to the educational process and the school knows what is in the best interest of students. Consequence is marginalized students' academic and personal/social needs are rendered even more invisible	Counselors and fellow educators view the counselor role to be protector of the status quo and does not question the over-representation of marginalized students in special needs classes, under-representation in gifted and talented programs, and over-representation in student discipline issues that result in suspensions and expulsions.	Counselors and fellow educators dismiss the notion the school has a prominent role in bridging achievement gaps and explains academic disparities being caused by forces external to the school such as student transiency, student culture, and/or low parental education.

Stephens, Diana L., & Lindsey, Randall B. (2011). *Culturally proficient collaboration: Use and misuse of scho*

Informed by Guiding Principles of Cultural Proficiency		
Cultural Precompetence	Cultural Competence—Informed by TSCI	Cultural Proficiency
Counselors and fellow educators foster an institutional and/or personal sense of responsibility for learning about cultural groups in the community. They learn how to disaggregate data in order to work with colleagues to interpret and plan for effective use of the data in ways that ensure student academic and personal/social success.	Counselors and fellow educators function as a team to access every classroom, working with teachers in selection and effective use of curricular content, and in facilitating classroom discussions that represent cultures of students in an inclusive manner. Students gain the knowledge and skills to negotiate problem solving situations and to access knowledge, skills, attitudes that serve them. *Counselor role is:* • Integral educational team member. • To foster teaming & collaboration. • Focused on mission & responsibilities.	Counselors and fellow educators organize in-school and community groups to address data in a way that incorporates divergent and often conflicting points of view as a catalyst for new ways of addressing and assessing efforts intended to meet the needs of all students, with particular attention to marginalized groups of students.

(Continued)

Table 4.1 (Continued)

Operational Definition of Essential Elements	Informed by Barriers to Cultural Proficiency		
	Cultural Destructiveness	Cultural Incapacity	Cultural Blindness
Institutionalizing Cultural Knowledge—the extent to which cultural knowledge is evident in counselor and fellow educator behavior and in school practices.	Counselors and fellow educators ascribe student behavioral issues as indicators of needing special education placement, which disproportionally affects historically underserved students. Counselors and fellow educators foster attitude denying any responsibility for exploring institutional barriers to teaching and learning. School counseling positions eliminated or drastically curtailed with justification of financial constraints. Eliminating counselors viewed as the least impactful to student academic achievement, which affects historically underserved students disproportionally.	Counselors and fellow educators view the primary role of the school counselor to help correct "deficiencies" in behavior that limit student success in school. Such actions often regard students' cultures as major impediment to their success in school.	Counselors and fellow educators fail to recognize and appreciate the role of culture in achievement gaps and how disparity impacts students' future career and personal/social success. Counselors and fellow educators limit the role of counselor to academic adviser.

Stephens, Diana L., & Lindsey, Randall B. (2011). *Culturally proficient collaboration: Use and misuse of scho*

Informed by Guiding Principles of Cultural Proficiency		
Cultural Precompetence	Cultural Competence— Informed by TSCI	Cultural Proficiency
School personnel beginning to regard evolving role of school counselor to include assessor of schoolwide student needs and not limited to provider of direct services. Counselors being included as collaborative member of leadership for instructional improvement with particular focus on achievement gap. Counselors serve as liaison between school & community/professional resources for determining culturally appropriate student support services.	Counselors and fellow educators structure opportunities for sharing expertise among school personnel. Counselors in conversation with all school personnel to provide updates on campus issues with structured time to brainstorm and set strategic plans to address areas of concern—data that highlight cultural/ demographic discrepancies that have impeded school responses to achievement gaps. *Counselor role is:* • Academic achievement promoter. To maintain focus on whole-school & system issues. • To keep primary focus of school on academic success.	Educators and school community view role of school counselor to be lead advocate for use of data to inform school of on-going successes and areas of continuous improvement as major components of systemic approach in serving the needs of a diverse student and community constituency.

Assumptions

The second activity asks you to analyze the rubric by reading beneath the vertical columns, Informed by Barriers to Cultural Proficiency and Informed by the Guiding Principles of Cultural Proficiency. You may want to follow these steps to guide your inquiry:

1. Read the 15 cells headed by Informed by Barriers to Cultural Proficiency and note the assumptions embedded in the descriptions and illustrations.

2. Summarize the assumptions for later reference.

3. Now read the 15 cells headed by Informed by the Guiding Principles of Cultural Proficiency and note the assumptions embedded in the descriptions and illustrations.

4. As with the previous step, summarize the assumptions.

5. Examine the two sets of assumptions. In what ways do they compare and contrast? What are your observations and reactions to the assumptions you have uncovered?

6. If conducting the activity with colleagues, compare and discuss your observations and reactions.

After completing these two activities, Verbs and Adjectives and Assumptions, you are now prepared to use the rubric in your own professional practice and with colleagues in service to your student population.

Uses of the Rubric

There are at least two uses of the rubric; one is inappropriate and the other is appropriate, useful, and productive.

- Inappropriate use of the rubric involves hearing a colleague make a comment or display a behavior that you can locate on the left side of the rubric and to inform them that you have demonstrable proof that they are Culturally Destructive, Culturally Incapacitous, or Culturally Blind. Although it may be tempting to point out such behavior, it neither leads to good relations with colleagues nor does it lead to change that benefits students.

- Appropriate use of the rubric begins with the same analysis as in the above illustration, but instead of making the other person the focus of your behavior, your focus is on what you do. For example, if the offending behavior is Culturally Destructive, you can use the rubric to examine options for what you say or do by reading the Culturally Precompetent, Culturally Competent, and Culturally Proficient illustrations.

- What we refer to as appropriate use of the rubric serves as an illustration of the inside-out approach of Cultural Proficiency.

The rubric provides formal and nonformal leaders a template for action. The rubric is not a stand-alone activity for school leaders, counselors, and their communities. The rubric is an action tool to assess progress toward clearly defined goals focused on improving student achievement. Effective use of the rubric as a leverage point for change is dependent upon deep-level conversations that emerge from using the four tools for cultural proficiency.

The reflective and dialogic devices presented in Part II, Chapters 5–9, are designed to facilitate deep-level thinking and conversations. For you the reader, the reflection activities provide the opportunity to think about your role as an educator and to *think about your thinking* when considering the cultures of your students. For your grade level, department, or school, the dialogic activities are designed to foster examination of school policies and practices that hinder or facilitate student access and achievement. As you proceed to Chapters 5–9, do so with anticipation for how consideration of your values and behaviors and your school's policies and practices will empower you as an educator.

Going Deeper

In what ways might the Counselor Collaboration Rubric: Misuse to Use help you and your colleagues as you consider and plan for change? How might it inform discussions about equity and access? Please use the space below to record your thoughts and questions.

_____

_____

_____

_____

_____

_____

PART II

Maple View— Sitting in the Fire

A Context for Culturally Proficient Counseling

Introduction to Part II

You are being invited and often challenged in this book to learn and apply the Essential Elements of Cultural Competence and the Transforming School Counseling Initiative's (TSCI) scope of practice. Chapters 5–9 describe one Essential Element each aligned with selected aspects of TSCI's 21st Century Role of School Counselor. It is important to note that the Five Essential Elements of Cultural Competence and TSCI's scope of practice are interdependent and do not exist in isolation. We chose to present them in separate chapters to facilitate study and mastery of the Five Essential Elements and the TSCI 21st Century Role of School Counselor. We are not suggesting a linear, one-for-one alignment of an essential element with a specific school counselor role. Rather we are presenting a holistic approach of essential elements and counselor roles.

The Five Essential Elements and the entire scope of practice of the 21st Century Role of School Counselor are brought together in Chapter 10 in a manner that is cohesive for the counselor, for school leaders, and for the school as an entity addressing achievement-gap issues. Chapter 10 offers the opportunity to mentor you in a way that provides the occasion to be reflective, action oriented, and proactive in using the new language of Cultural Proficiency yourself and with your colleagues. It is our intent that school counselors be integral members of school leadership teams focused on circumventing barriers to student access and academic success.

Sitting in the fire is a metaphor we use for people who have the courage and moral bearing to stay in a discussion, conflict, or sitting as an advocate for the best interest of our students. A generation ago, the term *gumption* was used to mean the same thing. Our colleagues Glenn Singleton and Curtis Linton (2006) rightly use the term "Courageous Conversations." Another way of representing such actions may be "'we are doing what is ethically responsible" as educators in addressing the academic, career, and personal/social future of our students. The descriptive information, vignettes, and reflections in Chapters 5–9 are crafted to describe the healthy language we can use in service of our students.

In the preceding chapters, you have read vignettes involving educators from the Maple View School District. Now, we formally introduce them to you, first in Table II.1 that lists the educators and their roles and the districts, and then we provide a brief narrative description of each educator.

Maple View School District

Last year the Maple View School District (MVSD) launched a five-year plan to restructure its approach to student support services and adopted the American School Counselor Association (ASCA) National School Counseling Program as a framework for school counseling programs. Dion, the Director of Student Support Services, structured a 3-day retreat, during which time leadership teams from each of the schools in the district worked collaboratively to develop a school counseling mission statement, identify their philosophy of practice as school counselors, and developed management agreements in how counselors would structure their use of time to provide comprehensive, developmental, results-based prevention and intervention programs to meet the needs of their respective school sites. Each counseling team conducted a program audit of their school-counseling program and a schoolwide needs assessment, identifying areas of alignment with the ASCA Elements and Domains, and areas of focus for their Year 2 of implementation.

A storyboard for the vignettes in this book, Resource A, is located in the Resources section. The storyboard summarizes by Essential Element the cultural issues presented, The Education Trust's Transforming School Counselor Initiative roles of counselor, the school setting within the MVSD, and the issues/action steps under consideration. The educators from MVSD are:

Dion, director of Student Support Services, a Pacific Island male has just met with the leadership teams in a 2-day retreat to report on progress during Year 1 and to establish strategic plans for further implementation of the school-counseling program. Through brain-storming with the teams and analysis of data collected during Year 1, the following areas were identified for focus in Year 2: Safety issues (e.g., bullying, violence, and gang affiliation); Personal and Social issues (e.g., selection and implementation of social-emotional curriculum); Achievement Gap (e.g., disparity in academic success based on ethnicity and socioeconomic status); and Access issues (e.g., special education, gifted and talented programs).

High School

Diego, the principal of Pine Hills High School, is a Latino male, and is in his second year as a high school principal. He spent four years as an elementary school principal and is relieved to be working with older students. He is known in the district as a "no-nonsense" guy, with clear expectation that rules are to be enforced and that students are to respect their elders. He is equally committed to ensuring that all school personnel understand that respect is to be earned based on how students are treated.

Michael, the head counselor of Pine Hills High School, is an African American male who was recently named the national School Counselor of the Year. He has been counseling for the past four years and quickly established himself as a leader and advocate on campus. His affable nature has endeared students and parents, especially families of color and families of students with special needs. He has won over skeptical teachers who were initially put off by his collaborative approach, his frequent request to attend their curriculum meetings, and his interest in giving presentations in their classrooms. Michael is committed to issues of social justice and continues to explore ways to develop a more inclusive culture in the school. It seems to him that far too many of the teachers live outside the school community and have never really understood the issues facing the students on campus.

Emilia, an English teacher at Pine Hills High School, is Latina. She is a compassionate teacher, a hard worker, and tries to develop a relationship with each of her students. She readily volunteers to work with the counseling team when they ask her input on how to more effectively establish connections with the other teachers. Her classroom is always open for counselors to observe her teaching style, and she is excited when they offer to conduct lessons that help her students.

Middle School

Stacie, the assistant principal at Pine View Middle School, is a white female. She was selected for this position because of her prior 10 years as a school counselor. She now leads the counseling team and required all counselors at her school site to attend the summer

Education Trust leadership retreat for school counselors. She is very direct in her expectation that her counseling team model best practices by implementing the ASCA national framework for school counseling programs

Flora, the counselor at Pine View Middle School, is a Native American female. She has been at this school site for the past 20 years. She worked 2 years as a teacher's aide, and then taught sixth grade for 10 years. She has stayed abreast of changes in the school counseling profession during these eight years as a school counselor. She is warm, methodical, and thorough in her interaction with students. She often serves as a site-supervisor for counseling interns and enjoys mentoring them into the field. She prides herself in her communication skills and her ability to facilitate meetings to help the assistant principal and teacher negotiate differences.

Ed, the eighth-grade history and science teacher at Pine View Middle School, is a white male. He is also a coach for after-school sports. He is a fun-loving guy, with a great sense of humor, and loves working in middle school. He is patient with his students and knows that they are more interested in their peer relationships than in learning about history and science. He tries to make his classes exciting by getting the students involved in projects. This is his third year at the school, and he is finally feeling he has found a "home" with his colleagues. He likes that the school counselor comes to his classes to talk about relationship building; he often learns as much as his students.

Elementary School

Gracie, the principal of Maple View Elementary School, is a white female. She is a new principal in her second year at the school. She feels insecure about her position, as she knows the staff, teachers, and counselor did not want to see their prior principal promoted to a district position. She feels burdened by the "big shoes" she is expected to fill. She believes the best way to approach the school is to set forth her expectations. She has reminded the counselor on a number of occasions that she is in charge, as it seems the counselor makes decisions without first getting her approval. As principal, she is worried that suspensions are increasing and the school's academic performance index (API) and adequate yearly progress (AYP) scores went down last year for the first time in the past six years.

Gabriella, the counselor of Maple View Elementary School, is a Latina. She is a part-time counselor at the school site and has been there for the last eight years. She is loved by all of the teachers and the staff. She is on a first-name basis with the parents and very involved with the community. She has a great sense of humor, and she is the first person called whenever a staff member or teacher has difficulty with a student. Gabrielle is often amused by how seriously adults respond to the antics of children. She continually reminds the adults to "chill out" and remember that they are here to teach not judge the children. She is having a difficult time coming back to school this year, as it was so tough last year to work with the new principal. She is still grieving the loss of the prior principal as they made such a good team in their work to provide resources to help all the students and to support the families in the community.

Sandy, the third-grade teacher at Maple View Elementary School, is a white female. She has worked at the school site for the past 12 years and would love to become an administrator working at the district level. She has her administrative credential and functions as the lead administrator when the principal is offsite. She is well liked by all the teachers and works closely with the counselor. She is also feeling the impact of working with this new principal who seems harsh and too directive. She wonders if the gains the school has made in their API and AYP scores are going to be impacted by the loss of collaboration.

Table II.1   Maple View Educators

School	Position	Name	Gender	Ethnicity
Maple View District Office	Director of Student Support Services	Dion	Male	Pacific Islander
Pine Hills High School	Principal	Diego	Male	Latino
	Counselor	Michael	Male	African American
	Teacher	Emilia	Female	Latina
Pine View Middle School	Assistant Principal	Stacie	Female	White
	Counselor	Flora	Female	Native American
	Teacher	Ed	Male	White
Maple View Elementary School	Principal	Gracie	Female	White
	Counselor	Gabriella	Female	Latina
	Teacher	Sandy	Female	White

Sitting in the Fire

Work described as *sitting in the fire* is what we are supposed to be doing as educators serving a diverse student population in a country based in democratic principles. Conversations such as these are referred to as courageous conversations, difficult conversations, or challenging conversations. Whatever moniker we use, we must explore within ourselves and in our schools what it will take to provide all students access to high-quality education. As you proceed to read the chapters that follow, keep these guidelines in mind:

- The guiding principles, our core values, keep us in the fire and represent the *inside-out* nature of the work.
- Reflection and dialogue are woven through Chapters 5–9 in three ways. First, the narratives and vignettes provide illustrations of reflection and dialogue *in practice*. Second, the reader is provided opportunity to reflect on their own values, beliefs, and practice and, then, the opportunity for meta-reflection and to "think about their own thinking." Third, readers are provided the opportunity to plan for using dialogic processes in their own school contexts.
- Chapters 5–9 are presented in a way that represents at least one of the Essential Elements of Cultural Competence in combination with one or more of the 21st century roles of counselors as framed by the TSCI.
- Each of the chapters will *sit in the fire* with one or more of the manifestations of systemic oppression present in society—racism, ethnocentrism, sexism, classism, heterosexism, ableism, and issues of faith/spiritualism or the absence thereof. These topics will be woven throughout the vignettes and accompanying narratives in each chapter.
- Examples:
  - Chapter 5, Assessing Cultural Knowledge—issues of ethnocentrism and English learning. In the vignette(s), the speakers will make reference to the guiding principles as their framework for the inside-out approach to their work.
  - Chapter 6, Valuing Diversity—heterosexism, and ableism. In the vignette(s), the speakers will make reference to the guiding principles as their framework for the inside-out approach to their work.
  - Chapter 7, Managing the Dynamics of Difference—ethnocentrism and classism. In the vignette(s), the speakers

will make reference to the guiding principles as their frame-work for the inside-out approach to their work.

o Chapter 8, Adapting to Diversity—sexism and racism. In the vignette(s), the speakers will make reference to the guiding principles as their framework for the inside-out approach to their work.

o Chapter 9, Institutionalizing Cultural Knowledge— heterosexism and issues of faith/spiritualism or absence thereof. In the vignette(s), the speakers will make reference to the guiding principles as their framework for the inside-out approach to their work.

Chapter 5 begins your inside-out journey to mastering the leader-ship role of the 21st Century School Counselor guided and informed by an Essential Element, Assessing Cultural Knowledge. In this chap-ter and each of the chapters through Chapter 9 you will read, think, and reflect on you and your role in school improvement. Take your time with each of the chapters and delve into the content, reflect on you and your school's practice, and formulate your thinking about current practices that are effective and specific areas for continued improvement. By the time you arrive at Chapter 10, you will be poised to address issues of equity, access, and student achievement in new and different ways.

5

Assessing Cultural Knowledge Through Leadership

We need to help students and parents cherish and preserve the ethnic and cultural diversity that nourishes and strengthens this community—and this nation.

—César Chávez (2010)

Getting Centered

Think about the schools you know—the schools you attended when you were a student, the school in which you teach or have taught, the schools your children attend, or the schools in your local community. If you are thinking of more than one of these schools, select only one for this activity. As you think of this school, how do you describe its academic culture? How do you describe the cultural involvement of the educators with the diverse communities the school serves? In what ways are counselors evident in leadership at the school? In what ways does the counselor assess and/or use his cultural knowledge relative to the community served by the school? Think about these questions, and use the space below to record your response to the questions that resonate for you.

_____

_____

_____

_____

With this chapter, we begin the introduction of the essential elements of Cultural Proficiency as standards for your professional educator behavior and for school policies and practices. The first essential element, *assessing cultural knowledge*, like the essential elements presented in Chapters 6–9, are derived from the guiding principles presented as core values in Chapter 3. Please read this and subsequent chapters in a way that allows you to absorb the manner in which the role of school counselor works with fellow educators to focus on and leverage equitable opportunities for all students.

We assume in your selecting to read this far that you are a school counselor, a fellow educator who recognizes the inherent value of school counselors as members of school leadership teams, or a layperson interested in education who is looking for ways in which to better serve all of our students' academic, career, and personal/social needs. In fact, you may be all of these people! In this chapter and the four that follow, you will be provided information and, as importantly, provided the opportunity to reflect on and think deeply about what you want formal and nonformal leaders to provide for the students in our schools.

Assessing Cultural Knowledge Through Leadership

Aligning the Essential Elements of Cultural Competence with the new, 21st century role of the Transforming School Counseling Initiative (TSCI) provides counselors with an integrated approach with leadership practices intended to serve all students equitably. Table 5.1 represents one essential element, Assessing Cultural Knowledge, aligned with leadership practices from the TSCI. When considered together, they represent a source of information for counselors and fellow educators serving the needs of a diverse student population. Take a moment and study Table 5.1; pay attention to the active voice in both the essential element and the practices of the new, 21st century role of school counselor.

Table 5.1 Assessing Cultural Knowledge Through Leadership	
Essential Elements of Cultural Competence	**TSCI 21st Century Counselor Role**
Assessing Cultural Knowledge	• Leader, planner, program developer • Involved with all stakeholders • To maintain academic focus on strengths

Assessing Cultural Knowledge

Introspection is a hallmark of an effective counselor. A counselor's ability to understand the relationship of his values to his behaviors relative to culture heightens his potential effectiveness in working with colleagues, students, and members of the community as he seeks to be ever more effective in diverse settings. Counselors who understand the limitations of their cultural knowledge are in a position to lead learning for themselves and others in ways that hold a high value for adult learning.

The first step in individual or organizational learning can be assessing the extent of knowledge we possess about our own culture, the cultures of the students who attend our school, and the cultures of the adults who work at the school. The second step can be to lead our schools to learn about the cultures in their community. As examples, suppose your school has an emerging new faith represented in your community such as Muslim or Baha'i or Wicca, where dress may be distinctive and different from the majority of students. How would you begin to learn what you know or do not know about the new group? An example of a concern arising in the community might be manifestations of ethnocentrism, where groups express belief in their cultural superiority. How would you go about learning what you know or do not know about such groups? How might you lead such learning with and for your colleagues?

A third step may be learning about the organizational cultures in your school's departments or grade levels. Paying attention to the organizational cultures within your school is useful information and serves as a way of leading learning in the school. If you are in an elementary school and attended a meeting of the second-grade team and then proceeded to the fourth-grade team, what differences might you notice in how business was conducted or in how people interacted? If you are in a secondary school, the question might be about the English and mathematics departments. Assessing cultural knowledge occurs when counselors initiate learning about others' cultures as assets, effective cross-cultural relationships, and about the school as a cultural entity focused on academic, career, and personal/social success. The new, 21st century role of school counselor facilitates school learning by providing leadership practices that deepen the school's attention to serving all students in an equitable fashion.

TSCI 21st Century Counselor Leadership Practices

Table 5.1 lists three leadership practices for the new role of school counselor—leader as planner and program developer; leader for involvement with all stakeholders; and, leader for academic focus on strengths. These practices and roles represent a major shift from the traditional role of school counselor as scheduler focused on individual interventions and ancillary services to one of direct interaction and coordination with administration, faculty, and community members focused on prevention support services and mutual accountability for students academic, career, and personal/social success.

Assessing Cultural Knowledge Through Leadership

The alignment of assessing cultural knowledge and leadership involves school counselors being mindful of their inside-out learning process, school culture, and facilitating the school's inside-out learning process about the community being served. Accessing cultural knowledge can be gained through reflective questions. In the section that follows are questions adapted from Lindsey, Jungwirth, Pahl, and Lindsey (2009). Take a few minutes to read the three sections that follow and construct reflective responses.

My Inside-Out Learning Process

- In what ways do I continue to learn about my own culture?
- In what ways do I learn about the cultures of our students?
- In what ways do I become aware of how I react to the cultures of the students?
- In what ways do I clarify my own beliefs about culture and diversity?

Reflections

Use the space below to record your responses to questions that spark a curiosity in you.

_____

_____

_____

_____

Facilitating My School's Inside-Out Learning Process About School Culture

- What might be some ways I/we learn about the organizational cultures that exist within the school (e.g., departmental, grade level, staff-faculty)?
- In what ways do we learn about the cultures of our students?
- In what ways do I develop support systems with administration and faculty toward specific goals?
- In what ways do I conduct and facilitate use of systemwide assessment surveys and data from Healthy Kids surveys to develop a counselor curriculum embedded in academic curricular content (e.g., study skills assessed early in the academic year)?
- In what ways do I/we plan and facilitate intentional professional learning, based on assessment surveys, to improve student learning?
- In what ways do I facilitate learning and using differentiated teaching strategies?
- In what ways does our learning community ensure assessing cultural knowledge is a lens for our work?
- In what ways do I foster learning about each other as faculty members and the unique learning needs within our adult learning community?
- In what ways do I facilitate sharing our understanding of our students' various cultures and their learning needs?

Reflections

Use the space below to record your responses to questions that spark a curiosity in you.

_____

_____

_____

_____

Facilitating My School's Inside-Out Learning Process About the Community We Serve

- In what ways do I become aware of how I react to the cultures of the parents, guardians, and foster care providers?
- In what ways do I/we learn how the educators and school are viewed from the cultural communities in the school area?
- In what ways do I advocate for student demographic groups, in ways that I can be heard by my colleagues, who have a history of not being represented in gifted and talented classes, overrepresented in special education classes, and are chronically lagging in academic achievement?

Reflections

Use the space below to record your responses to questions that spark a curiosity in you.

_____

_____

_____

_____

Using the Rubric

Assessing and Developing Cultural Knowledge Through Leadership

Now that you have an understanding of how Assessing Cultural Knowledge represents the inside-out learning process for you, your school, and your school's relationship with the community you serve, let's turn our attention to how leadership fosters assessing cultural knowledge. Let's begin our study with these two steps:

- Take a moment and refer back to Chapter 4, Table 4.1, Counselor Collaboration Rubric: Misuse to Use. Focus your attention on the first row of the rubric, Assessing Cultural Knowledge, and note the developmental aspects of the rubric when reading from left to right, from Cultural Destructiveness to Cultural Proficiency.

- Now turn your attention to Table 5.2 and note that it presents the Assessing Cultural Knowledge row of the rubric from Chapter 4. Two things to note:
  - Table 5.2 includes only the *positive* side of the rubric. However, in your role as a formal or nonformal leader, you will hear comments and become aware of practices represented on the left side of the continuum. The rubric is designed for the right side to provide choices when responding to comments/practices located on the left side represented as Cultural Destructiveness, Cultural Incapacity, or Cultural Blindness.

    Please be mindful that comments/practices may come from you and not always from colleagues and may, in fact, be

Table 5.2   Assessing Cultural Knowledge—New Role of 21st Century School Counselor

Five Essential Elements Informed by ASCA Domains • Academic • Career • Personal/ • Social Success	Cultural Precompetence	Cultural Competence—Informed by TSCI	Cultural Proficiency
Assessing Cultural Knowledge—extent to which counselors initiate learning about their own and others' culture(s) as assets and about the school as a cultural entity.	Counselors and fellow educators acknowledge gaps in own and colleagues' knowledge about student and community cultures as assets and assumes initiative to inform leadership team of need for self-study.	Counselors' role on leadership teams includes using the lens of educators' and students' personal culture and the schools' organizational culture as assets in providing responsive educational programs. *Role of counselor is:* • Leader, planner, program developer • Involved with all stakeholders • To maintain academic focus on strengths	Role of counselor viewed as catalytic advocate for social justice and lifelong learning for school personnel. Academic, career, and personal/social success of all students is primary and interdependent focus.

found on the left side of the rubric. As you become aware of comments/practices located at any point of the rubric, you can look to the illustrations on the right side of the rubric for suggested comments/practices for you and your colleagues. Wherever the comments/practices are found along the rubric, acknowledging their placement on the rubric represents the inside-out process of change for you and your school.

o As you read the entries for Cultural Precompetence, Cultural Competence, and Cultural Proficiency in Table 5.2, pay attention to adjectives and verbs, and note both the active voice and intentionality. What we are learning about the inside-out process for individuals and organizations is the need to be intentional in creating organizational change.

Effecting change for you and your school will be met with resistance by those who maintain that the students and their parents/guardians are the ones who need to conform to prevalent school practices. You may want to revisit the discussion in Chapter 3 about how the Guiding Principles of Cultural Proficiency provide the moral framework of Cultural Proficiency and informs the right side of the rubric. You will see in the vignette that follows that Gabriella models the inside-out approach to change for her and for the school. As you read the vignette, pay particular attention to evidence of progression along the rubric and how the moral framework is represented in the educator's actions.

Safe School Climate at Maple View Elementary School

The leadership team at Maple View Elementary School is meeting to assess progress in achieving their goal of creating a safer school climate, in the second year of their transforming school counseling initiative. Gabriella, the school counselor, and Sandy, the third-grade teacher, are sharing with their new principal, Gracie, facts about the school history and are identifying changes in the school. Take particular note of their discussion of the school's history and of the challenging discussions that must have occurred to make the progress they are enjoying. This conversation is an illustration of the benefits of *sitting in the fire,* related to the importance of equitable student achievement.

> **Gabriella—**You know, Gracie, it is amazing to reflect on how different our school is now, compared to when I first was hired as the school counselor a few years ago.
>
> **Gracie—**How is it different?

Gabriella—*Back then I called it the "brittle little school, very hard." I was actually afraid for my own safety. The fourth- and fifth-grade students actually scared me with their threatening posture and bullying. We faced a lot of disciplinary problems, and teachers were frustrated with all the interruptions to their teaching.*

Gracie—*That seems so hard to imagine given how much this school seems like a family—everyone pulls together.*

Gabriella—*We really worked as a team with some rather difficult questions, and new ways of looking at what was happening in the school.*

Gracie—*Like what?*

Sandy—*I remember, Gabriella, the day you asked in the staff meeting "How can we help our children be more cooperative in the classroom and on the playground?" That was the day I began to consider the challenge of discipline as a schoolwide issue.*

Gabriella—*That question wasn't easy for me to ask. For so long, I thought I was responsible for changing students' bad behavior. What I really needed help on was how to encourage students to focus on their academics and to be cooperative. We can't make academics and behavior oppositional. We were punishing them for their behavior, and yet I was wondering inside, "Are suspensions helping them academically?" I would leave school wondering, "Are we teaching them to treat one another with respect, or just expecting them to know how to do this? What was I missing here? Do they really know better, or are they doing the best they can?"*

Gracie—*What do you mean do they know better? I have to say I think that 9- and 10-year-olds know right from wrong.*

Gabriella—*I can appreciate that; many of us in the school held that view. I began to question, "How are my values and expectations influencing how I approach our students?" "Do I understand their cultural norms and expectations?" Maybe it would help to learn more about the students and one another.*

Gracie—*So what did you do?*

Gabriella—*Our leadership team worked together. We found an assessment instrument that focused on school climate and diversity, and sent it to the teachers, the staff, and the parents. That was a big shift for us, asking for one another's input.*

Sandy—*And an eye-opener! Remember how surprised we were about the results? Many of us had given up on our students.*

Gabriella—*I do remember, Sandy. The morale was down. We learned a lot from the survey about ourselves and our school, and how we blamed the parents and the families, saying that financial struggles and difficulty in communicating with parents who did not speak English stood in the way of teaching the children.*

Gracie—*What did you do with the information?*

Gabriella—*We had some further conversations together as a school. We also found some very positive qualities about one another and the parents. Most of us wanted to help our students and their families, and the parents wanted to be involved. We just didn't know how. What really broke our hearts was hearing from parents that felt no connection to the school. We didn't understand one another's culture and how that was impacting behavior. Here we were saying "they" were the problem, and these parents were feeling alienated.*

Sandy—*Our former principal shared this information with the whole school and the parents. We were all praised for our candor in the assessment. Then we pondered how do we change our school culture? How do we develop a support system for one another to engage our parents and to teach our children respect for one another?*

Gabriella—*That's what led to our schoolwide initiative to involve all of us learning together about one another and our impact on student success. Our principal supported my request to attend the cultural proficiency institute, and that is where I discovered that there was a new way to utilize counselors in transforming school cultures. I returned from that institute wondering, "How do we select and infuse social-emotional learning curriculum in our classrooms in ways that support the diverse needs of our students' academic achievement?"*

Gracie—*Wow—that's an inspiring story, I'm glad I asked. I had no idea of the journey, the history of how you developed such a caring school climate. I'm glad I'm part of the team now, too. But to be honest, as the new principal, I'm struggling a bit myself. I wonder, "How do I lead in a school that is so collaborative? How does my style of directing others fit in here? How will we know who's leading the way?"*

Sandy—*I appreciate your candor, Gracie. I'm still trying to grasp how to be a lead learner, and I've been wondering myself, "How can I better connect with our new principal?"*

Gracie—*This is a relief. It feels good to ask these questions out loud. So, let's think about this question together: "What conversations will help us all continue forward with ways to best serve our students, our parents, and our community?"*

Going Deeper

We began this chapter by having you reflect on your school experiences with particular attention to how you assess your knowledge of your culture(s), your knowledge about the organizational culture of your school, and the knowledge you and your fellow educators have about the communities you serve. In reading this chapter, in responding to the opportunities to reflect on practice, and reading the Maple View Elementary School story, you most likely have questions about yourself, your school, and your community that you may not have had prior to this reading. Please use the space below to record your *new* questions. They will guide your inside-out learning process about self, school, and community as they relate to assessing your cultural knowledge aligned with the leadership role of counselors.

_____

_____

_____

_____

_____

_____

6

Valuing Diversity
Through Advocacy

*My humanity is bound up in yours, for we can only be human
together.*

—Archbishop Desmond Tutu (2010)

Getting Centered

In this chapter we introduce and discuss *valuing diversity* as the second of the five essential elements. As you proceed through this chapter, the underlying core values represented in the guiding principles become evident in the behaviors represented as valuing diversity, in both individual behavior and in organizational policies and practices.

What thoughts come to mind when you read the quote above by Archbishop Desmond Tutu? Some of us might think about the work of religious personages or prominent civil rights leaders. Others of us might think in terms of race, gender, or social class issues important to us while yet others of us might think of political issues that either divide or unite communities and nations.

When thinking of you and your school's value for diversity, what comes to mind in terms of your educator colleagues? What comes to mind when you think of your school's value for diversity in terms of the custodians, secretaries, school grounds monitors, and teacher aides? Think about your students, your students' parents, guardians, or foster care providers and how your school values diversity among them. Now comes the challenging part—how would a visitor experience your school? How might a visitor spending a week with you be able to recognize you and your school's value for diversity for any combination of people mentioned in this paragraph? Take a moment or two to reflect then record in the space below your thoughts, reactions, or questions that occur to you as you consider these questions.

_____

_____

_____

_____

The Challenge of Valuing Diversity

Most likely you struggled a bit with the initial activity to identify, in unambiguous terms, how you and your colleagues value diversity in a manner that is apparent to all who meet and know you. Most people do struggle a bit with the activity. Rarely do we take the time or seize the opportunity to think about what a *value for* diversity looks like in our schools. We imagine that you described holidays and celebrations. We also expect that you included topics related to race, ethnicity, faith, and gender. You may have also described valuing diversity in terms of sexual orientation and/or ableness. Whatever your focus, it is our intent with this activity for us to think inclusively when considering our value for diversity. As Archbishop Tutu indicates, it is about *humanity*.

Archbishop Tutu's concept of humanity leads us to describe a dynamic of cultural conflict that some experience. As we discussed in Chapter 3, it is our experience that people invested with a belief in the inherent superiority of their culture(s) are conflicted with the guiding principles, in general, and core values such as valuing diversity, in particular, to be challenging. For such educators, valuing diversity becomes an act of compliance lacking in substance or commitment. Having a value for diversity means embracing the concept of culture that is embedded in the Guiding Principles of Cultural Proficiency. The guiding principles represent the moral framework for the work of Cultural Proficiency and the Five Essential Elements are the proactive voice of our behavior and our school's policies and practices.

Valuing Diversity Through Advocacy

Advocacy is at the heart of what effective educators have been doing since time immemorial. In the context of this book, an advocate is someone who believes that students can learn, that educators can teach, and that she will communicate those beliefs in ways that others can understand and act. So, aligning the Essential Elements of Cultural Competence with the new, 21st century role of the Transforming School Counseling Initiative (TSCI) is a way that provides counselors and other educators with an integrated approach to advocacy. Table 6.1 represents a second essential element, Valuing Diversity, aligned with advocacy practices from the TSCI. When considered together they represent a source of information and influence for counselors and fellow educators serving the needs of a diverse student population. The format of Table 6.1 will be familiar. Pay particular note to the active voice in both the essential element and the practices of the new, 21st century role of school counselor.

Table 6.1   Valuing Diversity Through Advocacy

Essential Element of Cultural Competence	TSCI 21st Century Counselor Role
Valuing Diversity	• Agent for change and equity • Champion for all students • Advocate for inclusion of all

TSCI 21st Century Counselor Advocacy Practices

Turn back to Table 6.1 again to note the three advocacy practices for the new role of school counselor—agent for change and equity, champion for all students, and advocate for inclusion of all. Just think what it might be like in your school if you had a designated advocate. Think about it for a moment. What might it be like if one or more educators functioned as the voice of the voiceless, the conscience for doing what is in the best interests of students, or the person who exhorted herself and other educators to continuous improvement in instruction and curriculum. Maybe you do. Advocacy, designated or not, can lead to increased participation among educators, parents and other community members, and students. It is through increased participation with the skillful leadership that counselors can provide that educational equity can be a mainstream focus for the school.

Valuing Diversity Through Advocacy

In this section you will deepen your understanding of the inside-out process of personal and organizational change focused on better serving students historically marginalized in our schools and society. First, let's examine the manner in which valuing, diversity, and advocacy are inextricably interlinked.

- Valuing begins with what we say or profess and proceeds to what we do and for what we are held accountable.
- Diversity recognizes the immutable, cultural makeup of our society.
- Advocacy holds that we educators are committed to the education of our students.

Then, it follows that to be congruent as a person, as an educator, and as an organization, educators and schools in a diverse society such as ours work in the best interest of all our students. When we are clear on the alignment of *valuing* and *advocacy*, the phrase from the preceding sentence "all of our students" need not be qualified or limited in any way. Our commitment, our job, is to learn how to educate all learners. The questions that follow are adapted from Lindsey, Jungwirth, Pahl, and Lindsey (2009) and are intended to support you as a reflective educator:

My Inside-Out Learning Process

- In what ways do I invite multiple perspectives?
- To what extent am I able to recognize a value for diversity within instructional strategies, formal and informal curricula, and assessment strategies?
- To what extent do I express a value for cultural groups even when they are not present in the room?
- In what ways do our students know my value for diversity?

Reflections

Take a moment to write notes to yourself about the questions—thoughts, reactions, or ponderings.

_____

_____

_____

_____

Facilitating My School's Inside-Out Learning Process About School Culture

- In what ways does our school support multiple perspectives?
- In what ways do we express our value for diversity by what we say and what we do?
- In what ways are our actions congruent with what we profess to value?
- In what ways do we express and acknowledge common purpose in student academic achievement and social success?
- In what ways do our students know that we, the adults at the school, value diversity?
- In what ways does our learning community ensure valuing diversity is a lens for our work?

Reflections

Now that you have the rhythm of this process, what comments do you have about the questions posed above?

_____

_____

_____

_____

Facilitating My School's Inside-Out Learning Process About the Community We Serve

- In what ways might our value for diversity be evident to parents, guardians, and foster care providers?
- In what ways do we involve parents, guardians, and foster care providers' voices' in discussion and decisions that affect their children?

Reflections

What are your thoughts and reactions as you read these questions? Do new questions occur to you?

_____

_____

_____

_____

Using the Rubric

Valuing Diversity Through Advocacy

Most likely you are now steeped in what the inside-out learning process means for you, your school, and your school's relationship with the community you serve. So, let's turn our attention to how advocacy supports valuing diversity. Let's continue our study with these two steps:

- Refer back to Chapter 4, Table 4.1, Counselor Collaboration Rubric: Misuse to Use. This time, turn your attention on the second row of the rubric, Valuing Diversity, and note the changing tone of the rubric when reading from left to right, from Cultural Destructiveness to Cultural Proficiency.
- Now look to Table 6.2 below, and note that it presents the Valuing Diversity row of the rubric from Chapter 4. Two things to note:
  - Table 6.2 includes only the *positive* side of the rubric. You will always be aware of practices represented on the left side of the continuum, but we don't want you to be stuck and responding inappropriately or walk away wishing you had said or done something. It is for occasions such as these that the rubric was designed. The right side of the rubric provides choices when responding to comments/practices located on the left side represented as Cultural Destructiveness, Cultural Incapacity, or Cultural Blindness. It is intended to move you from *stuck* to *unstuck*, to being proactive and sitting in the fire.

    As we indicated in the previous chapter, please be mindful that comments/practices on the left side of the rubric may come from you and not always from others. As you become aware of comments/practices located at any point of the rubric, you can refer to illustrations on the right side of the rubric for suggested comments/practices for you and your colleagues. The rubric may serve as an important aide in the inside-out process of change for you and your school.
  - Earlier in the book we introduced the concepts of *active voice* and *intentionality*. As you read the entries for Cultural Precompetence, Cultural Competence, and Cultural Proficiency, continue to pay attention to adjectives and verbs and note both active voice and intentionality. The inside-out process for individuals and organizations is about being intentional in creating organizational change.

Table 6.2   Valuing Diversity—New Role of 21st Century School Counselor

Five Essential Elements Informed by ASCA Domains • Academic • Career • Personal/ Social Success	Cultural Precompetence	Cultural Competence— Informed by TSCI	Cultural Proficiency
Valuing Diversity— extent to which informal and formal decision-making groups are inclusive of people whose viewpoints and experiences are different from the counselor and the dominant group at the school.	Counselors and fellow educators become aware of own and colleagues' limited knowledge about student cultures or the impact of negative school climate. Counselors are not sure how to access informal and formal decision-making groups within the school or community for information or support. Similarly, counselors don't know how to present such information to colleagues.	Counselors' role on leadership teams includes using the lens of educators' and students' personal culture and the schools' organizational culture as assets in providing responsive educational programs. *Role of counselor is:* • Agent for change and equity. • Champion for all students. • Advocate for inclusion of all.	Role of counselor viewed as catalytic advocate for social justice and lifelong learning for school personnel. Interdependence of academic, career, and personal/social success of all students is primary focus.

In our work with schools at all levels, preschools to universities, we experience resistance to change that involves serving all students equitably. Sometimes the resistance to change is active and hostile, but more often resistance is manifested by inertia. Whatever the source of resistance, the effect has the same impact on students labeled as *underperforming*. We argue these students are, in fact, underserved by the current educational system and need to be served differently. Having a moral bearing of doing what is right for students in your community guides you in moving the conversation from what is wrong with *them* to what is it that we need to learn in order to be more effective with more students. As you well know by now, we hold the guiding principles of Cultural Proficiency as providing a moral framework for guiding our actions. In the vignette that follows Ed, Flora, and Stacie are involved in the inside-out approach to change for them and for their middle school. As you read the vignette, note progression along the rubric and how the moral framework is represented in their actions.

Tragedy at Pine View Middle School

Pine View Middle School experienced a tragedy on campus last year two months before the end of the school year. Following a series of unacknowledged bullying events, a seventh-grade heterosexual male shot and killed a seventh-grade gay male classmate. This tragic event occurred on campus during the school day while classes were in session. Throughout the remaining days of the school year, a crisis trauma team assisted the school and the community to process the impact of this tragedy. The school leadership team met throughout the summer to support one another, to candidly discuss how this happened, and to explore a plan of action in building a culture of support and safety on campus. It is now three weeks before the start of the new school year. Stacie, the assistant principal; Flora, the school counselor; and Ed, an eighth-grade teacher are discussing their strategy and providing an illustration of *sitting in the fire* for doing what is in the best interest of students.

> Stacie—*I've been wondering how we can be proactive when we return to school, so we can be more effective in discussing bullying and harassment with our staff and faculty.*
>
> Ed—*I agree, we need to be proactive, though I wonder if conversing about bullying and harassment will be enough. Are we ready to support dialogue about sexual orientation, knowing that there are so many perspectives that might open up some strong reactions?*
>
> Flora—*I can appreciate what you are both asking. Perhaps we can broaden this conversation even more. I am going to be quite blunt here: "Do we have the moral courage to take our heads out of the sand"? Knowing that we have a very diverse population, are we prepared and willing to acknowledge that schools are the place to discuss gender, race, and discrimination of all sorts?*
>
> Ed—*Yikes—that is quite blunt.*
>
> Flora—*What I'm really trying to discuss is, how do we create a more inclusive atmosphere on campus so that the counseling office is not the only place that we*

talk about these issues? I know we are all aware that students are looking to us for help through the aftermath of a very traumatic situation last year. What can we do to acknowledge these personal and social issues that impact their learning and their grades?

Ed—Well, Flora, these are some tough questions that I believe we need to work through together. However, I have a nagging question in my own head that gets in the way of even considering what you are pondering.

Flora—What's that, Ed?

Ed—How did we fail both of these boys?

Stacie—Oh, wait a minute Ed! That's a pretty strong accusation—let's be careful what we say, and a little kinder to ourselves and to each another. It's not going to help to blame anyone.

Flora—I don't get the sense that Ed is trying to blame anyone Stacie—I hear this as a rhetorical question for our school, our community, and us.

Ed—Ok, I hear you. I didn't mean to muddy the waters. Let me try to put this in a more positive way. What can we do differently to serve all of our students so they know we value and embrace their diversity? I believe we can do better at this.

Flora—I agree, Ed. And just for the record, I don't think these two students were protected or helped like they should have been. And now one is dead and the other one might as well be. Most likely he will spend the rest of his life in jail, and he is only 13 years old! They were both just kids trying to deal with life the best they could.

Stacie—And we were doing the best we knew how at the time. Now our focus is on what we are going to do when school starts. We've talked about this all summer and I know our emotions still run high. I can only imagine how our students, faculty, and parents will feel when school opens. Are we united in our commitment to ensure that our staff and students are healing?

Flora—I believe so. We were attentive to our school needs after the shooting, and I have no doubt we will continue to offer services and referrals to all who need it. Now I wonder, are we ready to do more than grieve the loss we feel. Is this a wake-up call for us as a school and community?

Stacie—I think we can all agree on that point. We need to show more tolerance for others, even when we don't have the same beliefs or views. The question is, how do we get there?

Ed—Is it about showing more tolerance, or would it be better to show more respect for one another?

Flora—Well, I'd like to see us value the differences in each other, but our history is one of focusing on our similarities as if differences were invisible. We've got a great little school here, and a good district. Goodness knows we have already shown how to walk a new path that is more inclusive of all our needs.

Stacie—*In what way?*

Flora—*Though it was nowhere near the magnitude of the loss of these students, our "Healthy Children Initiative"—was a change that certainly stirred a lot of controversy.*

Ed—*Indeed it did—but we remained strong as advocates for tackling the obesity problem for our kids.*

Flora—*Oh yes, and the superintendent sure had our backs. Remember the parent and student protests when we took out the vending machines and stopped serving sodas and packaged meals?*

Stacie—*I sure do! It was a rough year. Then everything changed when we sent out the survey asking the students and parents what they liked about the new menu and what they wanted us to add?*

Flora—*Yeah—the kids like the fresh fruit and the parents complimented us on the healthy meals.*

Ed—*That's what I'm talking about. We can do this again. I've heard there are some good diversity programs out there, and Flora, I'm sure you can lead this initiative.*

Flora—*Well, I can get a conversation started, though I'm not an expert on diversity.*

Stacie—*None of us has to be. We can learn new ways together. Let's finish reading this material on cultural proficiency that Dion sent to us from the district office and take our concerns to the retreat. We don't have to solve these issues alone.*

Ed—*Great idea, Stacie. I sometimes forget that we have a lot of support with the other schools and the district.*

Flora—*That sounds good. Dion says that this next step with cultural proficiency will provide a way to deepen our conversations together.*

Stacie—*I am cautiously optimistic. Obesity is a national problem that gets lots of constructive media attention. Sexual orientation and murder are so much more explosive.*

Flora—*Hmmmm. That may be; however, we can no longer sidestep the issue. So, let's start thinking together. What might be some ways we can express our deeply held values for all our students—in all we say and do?*

Going Deeper

Hopefully you will never experience this type of tragedy in your school. Whether you do or not, students from historically marginalized demographic groups experience tragedy in the levels of undereducation they experience. Take this opportunity to jot notes to yourself. You may want to design the characteristics of a classroom, grade level or department, or school that values diversity and where advocacy is a shared norm. You may want to reflect on the levels of tragedy exemplified in the vignette and write what you would have wanted to do or say had you been Ed, Flora, or Stacie. You may want to record your thoughts and feelings. The space below is for you to use.

_____

_____

_____

_____

_____

_____

7

Managing the Dynamics of Difference Through Teaming and Collaboration

Probably the foremost intellectual behavior for postindustrial society will be a heightened ability to think in concert with others.

—Senge et al. (2000, p. 204)

Getting Centered

In this chapter, we add the essential element *managing the dynamics of difference* to the two already introduced, *assessing cultural knowledge* and *valuing diversity*. With this chapter you will have studied three of the five standards for educator behavior and school's educational practices that we use in our work. By this point in the book, you are becoming increasingly aware that Cultural Proficiency is composed of four tools and that the guiding principles serve as core values that give rise to the essential elements as standards on which we build personal and organizational practice.

Take a moment and think about your educator colleagues. Have you had occasion in the last two years to experience you or your colleagues complaining that some of the students just don't seem to be able to work together well?" If so, in what ways did you or your colleagues respond? How would you have liked to respond? Please use the space below to record your thinking.

_____

_____

_____

_____

Managing the dynamics of difference introduces the concepts of problem-solving, conflict resolution, and mediating differences as important skills for use in any organization and, in particular, organizations that hold culture as a high value. In making the statement that serves as the epigraph for this chapter, Senge and colleagues (2000) continue by noting that our students may need to be taught how to work effectively in groups. We believe, in many cases, the same holds true for we who are the adults in schools. They refer to our students by saying, "They (i.e., students) may exhibit competitiveness, narrowness of viewpoint, egocentrism, ethnocentrism, and criticism of others' values, emotions, and beliefs" (2000, p. 204).

Managing the Dynamics of Difference Through Teaming and Collaboration

School counselors have always served an important role in school faculties and now, with the emergent role of the 21st century role of the Transforming School Counseling Initiative (TSCI), the focus on counselor becomes more pronounced. The counselor is one who supports team formation and development and initiates collaboration among constituent groups within the school and with the community to leverage change that benefits students equitably. The intersection of teaming/collaboration with the essential element _managing the dynamics of difference_ is propitious in that the communication, problem-solving, and conflict resolution skills honed by the novice or experienced school counselor alike support teaming and collaboration. Table 7.1 presents the essential element alongside the practices of the new, 21st century role of school counselor.

Table 7.1	Managing the Dynamics of Difference Through Teaming and Collaboration

Essential Element of Cultural Competence	TSCI 21st Century Counselor Role
Managing the Dynamics of Difference	• Broker of school-community resources • Data user for change agenda • Team leader accountable for student success

Managing the Dynamics of Difference

Unfortunately, too often terms such as difference, conflict, problems, and even diversity carry negative connotations. Difference is as normal in nature or organizations as is similarity. Conflict and problems are part of the ordinary order of living, too. Schools are a place where we come together to equip our students with knowledge and skills to navigate life, and we are adept at letting them know how big and complicated is life. From preschool through high school, our students are imbued with the notion that there are thousands of different animals, more than 100 countries, numerous types of music, multiple perspectives, and varied approaches to life and living. We teach our students how to make friends, to add and subtract, to play musical instruments, to solve simple to complex math equations, and to travel throughout the world. As educators, our curricula reflect a shared value for difference, conflict and solving problems. Diversity is required in nature and in organizations.

However, very often as adults when confronting issues of cultural difference, we find ourselves not recognizing or confronting our own feelings about cultural differences, avoiding intervening to deal directly with issues that arise out of cultural differences among our colleagues, or turning a blind eye to concerns that arise from cultural communities that feel marginalized in our educational processes. The rise of the accountability movement in this first decade of the 21st century is presenting us with an opportunity to bring our knowledge and skills about difference front and center to our educational practice, whether we are a counselor, administrator, teacher, aide, secretary, custodian, or parent/guardian. The accountability movement has made the achievement gap visible in unprecedented ways that many educators and schools are turning to their advantage. Because of the presence of disaggregated data, we are presented the opportunity to discuss our students in terms of their cultural groupings—by race/ethnicity, gender, and socioeconomic status. Across the country, educators and parents/guardians are discussing student access and achievement in the context of student demographic groups and are assessing effective and ineffective interventions. By doing so, they are selecting and implementing instructional strategies, assessment techniques, grade-level configurations, curriculum, and cocurricular options for students informed by their knowledge of what is best for students. By knowing and respecting the cultural assets students bring to school, we avoid having a narrow educational program tailored for the hypothetical *typical* student, which historically has been middle-class America.

TSCI 21st Century Counselor as Team Member and Collaborator

Table 7.1, Managing the Dynamics of Difference Through Teaming and Collaboration, presents three practices for the new role of school counselor—broker of school-community resources, data user for school change, and team leader accountable for student success. It is in this new version of the role of school counselor where he has the opportunity to use his communication, problem-solving, and conflict resolution skills in a way that will touch many students. The counselor who works through faculty and parents/guardians to identify and deploy school and community resources, to guide discussion and use of data that focuses on student access and success, and to facilitate an understanding of different viewpoints is an asset to all in the school community.

Take a moment and think about your school. If you were made *monarch for the year* in terms of student access and success, what issues are not being addressed at your school that need and should be addressed? What do you believe to be the impediments to those issues being addressed responsibly? Hold those thoughts as you read further in this chapter.

Managing the Dynamics of Difference Through Teaming and Collaboration

We have inferred from Senge and colleagues (2000) that narrowness of viewpoint, egocentrism, ethnocentrism, and other such filters impede people working together for a common good. Cultural Proficiency's inside-out approach to personal and organizational change is intended to confront such impediments or barriers. In Chapter 6, we discussed the importance of introspection and valuing diversity to being an effective educator in a diverse society. Diversity brings with it similarity and difference, the latter, which can create stress. Our role as educators is to equip our students with knowledge and skills for being able to manage and negotiate difference as a necessary part of the learning process. Even when our schools appear to be culturally homogeneous, we are preparing students to enter and be responsible citizens in an increasingly diverse society.

The linkages among managing the dynamics of difference and teaming/collaboration are fundamental to any learning organization. The manner in which these concepts are related in a school addressing issues of equity and access include the following:

- Managing the dynamics of difference acknowledges that difference exist among us and what is required is the manner in which we acknowledge, then, facilitate and foster an understanding of one another's viewpoints or positions.
- Teaming acknowledges that schools comprise grade-level and departmental configurations. The extent to which these entities function as teams may be directly related to the ability of members to express and hear one another's viewpoints.
- Collaboration is the basis for believing that the sum of the whole is greater than any of its parts. Throughout our schools we hold in high esteem collaboration, and thereby, teaming—as students line up to move from room to room, on the football or soccer field, in the school drama productions, with the science fairs, cheer teams, tech teams, and other team experiences.

Models of managing the dynamics of difference, of teaming, and collaboration are extant among the effective work we do with our students. Our task, then, is transferring the values and skills inherent to managing the dynamics of difference, teaming and collaboration to productively address issues of access and success for our students' academic, career and personal/social success. We have adapted the questions below from Lindsey, Jungwirth, Pahl, and Lindsey (2009) to support you and your colleagues as we all continue our journey to be reflective educators.

My Inside-Out Learning Process

- In what ways do I know of my cultural biases, and how they might be reflected in my role as an educator?

- In what ways do I foster alternative narratives in my work as an educator working with students?

Facilitating My School's Inside-Out Learning Process About School Culture

- In what ways do we foster alternative narratives in the classroom and in the formal curriculum?
- In what ways are our decision-making processes transparent and subject to change based on community needs?
- In what ways do we use assessment data to inform successful and unsuccessful practices?

Facilitating My School's Inside-Out Learning Process About the Community We Serve

- In what ways do we foster discussions about race, gender, sexual orientation, socioeconomics, and faith as related to the needs of our community?
- In what ways do we foster alternative narratives in parent and community meetings?

Reflections

Use the space below to record your thoughts, comments, and questions as you consider these questions and those posed earlier in this section.

Using the Rubric

Managing the Dynamics of Difference Through Teaming and Collaboration

At this point in the book you are experienced in using the rubric from Chapter 4 to guide your inside-out approach to your and your school's learning. Our focus in this chapter is the third row of the rubric, the essential element *managing the dynamics of difference* informed by teaming and collaboration. We recommend these steps for your consideration:

- Turn to Chapter 4, Table 4.1, Counselor Collaboration Rubric: Misuse to Use. Look to the third row of the rubric, managing the dynamics of difference, and be mindful of the changing tone of the rubric as you read from Cultural Destructiveness to Cultural Proficiency.
- Take a moment and examine Table 7.2 below and note that it presents the Managing the Dynamics of Difference row of the rubric from Chapter 4. Please note two things:
  - Table 7.2 includes only the *positive* side of the rubric. Negative practices on the left side of the continuum will always be there, but for our purposes here, we focus to the right side of the rubric, where illustration for responding to comments/practices represented as Cultural Destructiveness, Cultural Incapacity, or Cultural Blindness. It is intended to move you from being stuck with thoughts such as *I wish I had not been silent and had spoken up,* or *I didn't know what to say for fear of being misunderstood,* or *hey; it's no big thing.* It is our belief that being stuck is a *big thing,* and the right side of the rubric provides a frame for moving your internal thoughts to productive actions for you, your school, and the students in your school.

    Once again, please be mindful that comments/practices on the left side of the rubric may come from you and not always from others. As you become aware of comments/practices located at any point of the rubric, you can refer to illustrations on the right side of the rubric for suggested comments/practices for you and your colleagues. The rubric may serve as an important aide in the inside-out process of change for you and your school.
  - *Active voice* and *intentionality* are hallmarks of the culturally competent/proficient educator. As you read the entries for Cultural Precompetence, Cultural Competence, and Cultural Proficiency, continue to pay attention to adjectives and verbs and note both active voice and intentionality. The inside-out process for individuals and organizations is about being intentional in creating organizational change.

Table 7.2   Managing Dynamics of Difference—New Role of 21st Century School Counselor

Five Essential Elements Informed by ASCA Domains • Academic • Career • Personal/ • Social Success	Cultural Precompetence	Cultural Competence— Informed by TSCI	Cultural Proficiency
Managing the Dynamics of Difference— the extent to which counselors use problem-solving and conflict strategies as ways to be inclusive of multiple perspectives.	Counselors and fellow educators begin to collaborate in developing within academic curricular content personal-social areas that increase potential for life-long success of students.	Counselors and educator colleagues conduct data examination sessions within the school and with constituents to foster discussions that surface divergent perspectives in a manner that addresses demographic groups of students who have been marginalized within the school culture. *Role of counselor is:* • Broker of school-community resources. • Data user for change agenda. • To be accountable for student success.	Counselors work with other educators and community members to address equity issue disparities at all levels of governance— local, district, state, and with educators' professional organizations.

Access Issues at Pine Hills High School

The leadership team at Pine Hills High School is reviewing achievement and discipline data from last year to get a sense of student progress and to identify areas where increased student support services are needed. Michael, the lead counselor, has already met with his counseling team to analyze enrollment patterns in advanced placement classes and to explore behavior issues that resulted in suspensions. Michael is pleased to be at the table with his colleagues using data to inform their decisions. Not so long ago, Michael was not involved in these discussions since counselors at that time were not members of the leadership team. What a change he has seen in these last three years since he first approached his principal! He began to influence Diego's perception of his role by asking to attend a summer leadership workshop at The Education Trust on data-informed decision-making for counselors. Now, both Michael and Diego understand the importance of achievement data, and Michael more clearly sees his role in accountability for student success and is willing and prepared to *sit in the fire* to the extent necessary to make this discussion central to the school's concerns. Today, Michael is discussing with Diego, the principal, and Emilia, the English teacher, concerns about current school policies regarding selection of students for advanced placement classes.

> **Michael**—*Looking at these enrollment patterns is quite revealing.*
>
> **Diego**—*How so?*
>
> **Michael**—*There are some significant disparities in ethnicity between who gets into our advanced placement classes and who doesn't.*
>
> **Diego**—*We have a clear policy on this, Michael, and ethnicity isn't involved. Eligibility is based on performance.*
>
> **Emilia**—*Yes, it is. All students are eligible based on their grades. If you make the grade, you make the class.*
>
> **Michael**—*I'm wondering about the history of this policy and its current applicability. Is it equitably serving the needs of all students in our school?*
>
> **Diego**—*What's your point, Michael?*
>
> **Michael**—*Well, I've been researching perspectives on student achievement. I've learned that grades don't tell the whole story about a student's ability. I'm just concerned that we are falling into a pattern of creating barriers for our students by basing our decisions on GPA and not looking any deeper. Have we considered permitting all of our students' access to the rigorous curriculum of AP classes?*
>
> **Diego**—*So more can fail? Are you suggesting we put students in AP classes who aren't making the grades? Not everyone is cut out for these classes.*
>
> **Michael**—*Maybe our thinking has not kept pace with current data? Or perhaps our own worldviews are clouding the issue and contributing to students lagging behind?*

Emilia—*Michael, what are you saying?*

Michael—*It's not what I'm saying; it's what our data are showing. In looking at the demographics of students in our AP classes, the majority of them are Asian and white. It's been that way over time, and I'm wondering what that is showing us about equal opportunities for our Latino and African American students? Though they represent 55% of our school population, only 2% of them are in AP classes. Are we saying they are not as capable?*

Emilia—*Of course not!*

Diego—*I get where you are coming from, Michael, and I must say the data doesn't look too good for the school. I am aware of this disparity in achievement in our nation; Latino and African American students are underperforming in many schools—that's what the achievement gap is all about.*

Michael—*I wonder if they are underserved or need to be served differently in our school? Are we providing them the resources to be successful? Maybe it's an opportunity gap as much as an achievement gap?*

Diego—*Powerful questions, Michael. My question is, aren't they underserved in society and our schools just receive this "unfairness"? How do we respond in a more equitable way in school when life isn't fair? Many of these students come from very meager circumstances; their home lives certainly impact school performance. When you don't have enough food on the table, your family doesn't speak English, or you live in a dangerous neighborhood always looking over your shoulder, what can you expect? Aren't they doing the best they can?*

Emilia—*Diego has a point here. I don't like it, Michael, and I appreciate your concern, because it isn't fair or equal to these students. But, isn't this a larger problem than we can solve? We are just a school, doing the best we can. We have great teachers and leaders, and I know we all care.*

Michael—*I believe we care, too. I wonder if we are willing to explore our own cultural beliefs and practices? Are we buying into myths like "conditions of poverty make students less capable of academic success" or "if students are African American or Latino they must come from 'unfortunate circumstances'"? Though we can't change societal hurdles, can we do more to ensure that our school is a safe and welcoming place for students that foster access to the highest levels of curriculum? Would it help our students if we reflected more on our teaching style and identified what would improve student achievement?*

Emilia—*You are just full of questions today, Michael.*

Michael—*Perhaps so. Examining these data has changed my perspective. Even our suspension rates reflect gender and ethnic disparities. I'm not trying to point fingers; I want us to come together in this so we can do what is right and make a difference.*

Diego—*Thanks, Michael, I appreciate your comments. I'm feeling a bit defensive, so, maybe I'm too hard on my community, let me try to put that aside. Is there something you believe we can do to help?*

Emilia—*Yeah, I'm all on board with helping more. Is there something you have in mind, Michael?*

Michael—*Thanks for sticking with me and listening. I'm wondering how can we create more equitable access to resources so all of our students are successful? There are schools doing this and they are willing to share how they have turned around their schools to serve all students. Would we considering collaborating with them to learn more effective practices?*

Emilia—*How do we find out about these schools?*

Michael—*We can start by taking a look at the College Board website. They are in partnership with The Education Trust in closing the achievement gap. I was just reading one of their latest reports identifying states and schools across America that have increased access and achievement for Latino and African American students.*

Diego—*I think I'm catching on to what you are saying, Michael. Good thinking.*

Emilia—*I like that, too. But I'm still thinking about your comment that we need to examine our beliefs. Maybe that's another part of the issue.*

Michael—*Yeah. I appreciate that we can hang in there together because these are not easy conversations. A question we might consider is how our cultural biases may be reflected in our practice as a counselor, in my case, or as teacher and administrator?*

Diego—*That's another good thinking question. I am impressed with the quality of questions that have surfaced today. I'm also wondering, what can we do as a school to help all of our students experience academic success? I'd like you to bring these data to the cultural proficiency retreat, Michael. It's a good place to expand our conversation.*

Going Deeper

When thinking about the rubric in Table 7.2 and the Pine Hills High School vignette, in what ways has your thinking about your educational practice and that of your school/district been informed? What cultural issues are being addressed? What do you see as successes in addressing the issues? Have any of the issues been with your school for a decade or more? If so, why do you think that to be the case? If the adults at the school using current resources could do two things that would improve student access and success, what might those be?

_____

_____

_____

_____

_____

_____

8

Adapting to Diversity Through Counseling and Coordination

Poor people do not cause poverty any more than enslaved human beings caused a system of institutionalized slavery.

—Sue Books (2004, p. 9)

Getting Centered

Take a few moments to think about your life, including and beyond your role as an educator. Remember when you first met a person who was to become an integral, positive part of your life. You may recall a time when you first met your lifelong partner or another best friend, or the spouse of your parent, or an adult that was to be your parent/guardian. Whoever it is to be, take a few moments and remember how you were influenced by having this person in your life and the changes and adjustments you (and most likely) they made as a consequence of being in one another's lives. Use the space below to record two or three ways in which you and this person made changes to be in one another's lives. What reactions and feelings do you associate with the changes that occurred for you?

_____

_____

_____

_____

In this chapter we add _adapting to diversity_ to the essential elements already presented in Part II, _assessing cultural knowledge, valuing diversity_, and _managing the dynamics of difference_. These elements serve as standards for our behavior and our schools' practices. We also remind you that the Essential Elements of Cultural Proficiency are foundational in the core values implicit in the Guiding Principles of Cultural Proficiency, another of the Tools of Cultural Proficiency.

Though the guiding principles serve to inform each of the five essential elements comparably, their relationship to _adapting to diversity_ is similar to the previous elements in that we actually _do_ something. Adapting to diversity is not an abstract concept; it suggests that we adjust our practice, as an educator and as a school, to those with whom we work and not vice versa.

Adapting to Diversity Through Counseling and Coordination

Counselors have a unique leadership role in our schools that can coordinate the considerable talent of the school. Table 8.1 features the essential element of adapting to diversity within the new, 21st century role of the Transforming School Counseling Initiative (TSCI). Please note the functions—coordinates the educational team, coordinates teaming and collaboration, and coordinates a focused mission with responsibilities. The counselor uses her role and skills to coordinate two macrofunctions:

- To focus the school's organizational diversity on purpose of schooling, namely the education of students. The education of students is our sole reason for being in school (virtual or otherwise).
- To focus the school's responsibility to educate all students equitably. In doing so, the counselor assists and supports her colleagues to be mindful of the assets their students possess and not to pine for the students who used to be there or ones who they wished were there now.

Table 8.1 Adapting to Diversity Through Counseling and Coordination

Essential Element of Cultural Competence	TSCI 21st Century Counselor Role
Adapting to Diversity	• Coordinates educational team • Coordinates teaming and collaboration • Coordinates a focused mission with responsibilities

Adapting to Diversity

This essential element adds the aspect of adaptation to our on-going discussion of diversity as adapting connotes educators becoming increasingly effective in cross-cultural interactions and situations. Educators who recognize the assets possessed by the communities, cultures, and students they serve are well prepared to make affirmative steps. Similarly, educators who recognize and adjust to the diversity of cultures and organizational approaches within the school are positioned to be effective working with colleagues. Adaptation can be a sign of respecting others' cultures through being willing and able to learn from and with people who experience the world differently from you and who may approach tasks differently than you do.

Adapting to diversity sends the very clear message that you do not exude an air of superiority, either regarding your own cultural membership or in how you work with others. Educators who adapt to diversity continually engage in reflection and dialogue as fundamental ways in which they experience their personal and professional lives.

TSCI 21st Century School Counselor as Coordinator

Schools are complex organizations serving the needs of students, educators, classified staff, and members of the community. The school counselor as a nonformal school leader engages in coordination practices that support the academic and social purposes of schooling. Effective counselors coordinate the team function of schooling and collaboration with a focus on the school's mission that clearly delineates each educator's responsibilities.

In the role of coordinator, school counselors are mindful of the multiple resources needed to best support the diverse needs of students, and the limitations of time in which students may access support without interrupting in-class teaching. Counselors coordinate services to be provided before school, during lunch periods, after school, and in the evenings. Counselors play a pivotal role in navigating differences in school hours and the working schedules of parents, and guardians, to coordinate opportunities for student access to resources and parental connection to schools. Counselors serve as a liaison, identifying potential professional development training for faculty and staff to enhance their learning about student needs and coordinating schoolwide initiatives aimed at creating safe and caring school climate.

Adapting to Diversity Through Coordination

The intended impact of counselors' coordinator function is for faculty and students alike to be receptive to learning about the cultures in the school community to enhance students' academic and personal success. Learning about and esteeming others cultures provides educators and students knowledge, values and skills important to our diverse society. Through living these attitudes and skills, educators and students alike are more able to integrate divergent views and conflicting points of view in ways that addresses underlying and often intractable barriers to student success. The process of adaptation is fundamental to the inside-out process of change for people and their organizations.

Combining the coordinator function of school counselor with adaptation to diversity carries with it the opportunity for all educators to use the skills of reflection and dialogue for schools to productively address issues of access and success for our students' academic, career, and personal/social success. The questions below are adapted from Lindsey, Jungwirth, Pahl, and Lindsey (2009) to support you and your colleagues as we all continue our journey as reflective educators.

My Inside-Out Learning Process

- In what ways am I informed by multiple and alternate perspectives?
- In what ways do I develop adaptive practices to support newcomer and veteran community members?
- In what ways do I stay informed about the changing demographics of our school and community?

Reflections

Think about your role in this school and respond for how you view your role at school. Please use the space below to record your comments.

_____

_____

_____

_____

Facilitating My School's Inside-Out Learning Process About School Culture

- In what ways do I model appropriate communication skills to allow for multiple voices and experiences?
- In what ways do I support the school's learning about the changing demographics of the school and community?
- In what ways do I incorporate cultural knowledge into school discussions, irrespective of the demographic composition of deliberating group?
- In what ways does our school advocate for equity when resources are limited?

Reflections

Think about your role in this school and respond for the manner in which you work with others.

_____

_____

_____

_____

Facilitating My School's Inside-Out Learning Process About the Community We Serve

- In what ways are we intentional in learning about the cultural composition of our community?
- What are some ways we extend the learning of educators into the community?

- In what ways do we support community members learning about the changing demographics of our community?

Reflections

Think about your role in this school and describe the manner in which you work with others.

_____

_____

_____

_____

Using the Rubric

Adapting to Diversity Through Counseling and Coordination

By now, you are fully aware the rubric from Chapter 4 is designed to guide your inside-out approach to your and your school's learning. The focal point in this chapter is the fourth row of the rubric, the essential element *adapting to diversity* informed by counseling and coordination. Consider these steps to guide reading the rubric:

- Turn to Chapter 4, Table 4.1, Counselor Collaboration Rubric: Misuse to Use. Read the fourth row of the rubric, adapting to diversity, and note the changing tone of the rubric as you read from Cultural Destructiveness to Cultural Proficiency.
- Table 8.2 below presents the Adapting to Diversity row of the rubric from Chapter 4. Please keep these in mind as you read:
  - Table 8.2 includes only the positive side of the rubric. In the real world, the negative practices on the left side of the continuum are noticeable for their ubiquity, but for our purposes, we focus to the right side of the rubric, where illustration for responding to comments/practices represented as Cultural Destructiveness, Cultural Incapacity, or Cultural Blindness. It is intended to move you from being mired in thoughts such as *I won't deal with those bigots*, or *I am concerned about what they could do to me*, or *I can last to the weekend and be away from all this for a couple of days*. It is our belief that being *stuck*

(Text continues on page 125.)

Table 8.2   Adapting to Diversity—New Role of 21st Century School Counselor

Five Essential Elements Informed by ASCA Domains • Academic • Career • Personal/ Social Success	Cultural Precompetence	Cultural Competence—Informed by TSCI	Cultural Proficiency
Adapting to Diversity— extent to which cultural knowledge is integrated into the values of the counselor and fellow educators and into the policies of the school.	Counselors and fellow educators foster an institutional and/ or personal sense of responsibility for learning about cultural groups in the community. They learn how to disaggregate data in order to work with colleagues to interpret and plan for effective use of the data in ways that ensure student academic and personal/ social success.	Counselors and fellow educators function as a team to access every classroom, working with teachers in selection and effective use of curricular content, and in facilitating classroom discussions that represent cultures of students in an inclusive manner. Students gain the knowledge and skills to negotiate problem-solving situations and to access knowledge, skills, and attitudes that serve them. *Role of counselor is:* • Integral educational team member. • To foster teaming and collaboration. • Focused on mission and responsibilities.	Counselors and fellow educators organize in-school and community groups to address data in a way that incorporates divergent and often conflicting points of view as a catalyst for new ways of addressing and assessing efforts intended to meet the needs of all students, with particular attention to marginalized groups of students.

is important to recognize and acknowledge and to use the right side of the rubric as a lens for moving your internal thoughts to productive actions for you, your school, and the students in your school.

To reinforce previous cautions, please be aware that comments/practices on the left side of the rubric may come from you and not always from others. As you become attentive to comments/practices located at any point of the rubric, you can use illustrations on the right side of the rubric as the basis for comments/practices for you and your colleagues. The rubric may serve as an important resource in the inside-out process of change for you and your school.

o *Active voice* and *intentionality* are characteristic of the culturally competent/proficient educator. As you read the passages for Cultural Precompetence, Cultural Competence, and Cultural Proficiency, continue to pay attention to adjectives and verbs and note both active voice and intentionality. The inside-out process for individuals and organizations leads to intentional organizational change.

Pregnancy as an Access Issue at Pine Hills High School

The counseling team at Pine Hills High School is moving along well in discussing the Essential Elements of Cultural Proficiency in relationship to transforming their school counseling program. Michael, the head counselor, has been working with his counseling team to examine policies that impede student access to rigorous curriculum. Michael was particularly concerned about the number of pregnant females of color who were transferred to an alternative education program, thus compromising the young women's academic opportunities. Michael recently learned from Emilia that one of her students, Jasmine, is in jeopardy of losing her spot in advanced placement classes because she is pregnant. Diego, the principal, met with Jasmine and her parents, encouraging them to transfer her to Elmwood Academy, the local continuation school that has a pregnant minor program. Michael suggested a three-way consultation with Emilia and Diego, noting that they all have responsibility in helping Jasmine. Let's listen in on their conversation and pay particular attention to how these colleagues *sit in the fire* and recognize the underlying tensions, but keep focused on issues of equity and access.

Emilia—*How can we ask Jasmine to give up all she has achieved here at Pine Hills and transfer to Elmwood Academy? She is one of our brightest and highest achieving 11th-graders in advanced placement classes!*

Diego—*I don't see it as her giving up what she has achieved. She can continue her excellent performance and graduate on time. Elmwood has a very successful graduation rate.*

Emilia—*Elmwood doesn't have a rigorous curriculum, and there are no AP classes. How does she maintain her competitive edge and continue on target for a scholarship to a prominent university?*

Diego—*Let's get real here. Jasmine's life is changing forever, so how is a scholarship her priority now? She can benefit from Elmwood's pregnant minor program. We can't provide her the same support and services here at Pine Hills.*

Emilia—*I've talked with Jasmine and she asked me directly, "Can I stay here at Pine Hills?" How do we tell her no?*

Diego—*I encourage all of us to support this transfer. What we can do is guide her in making the best decision for now. She can return here for her senior year. In the meantime, she can bond with other girls at Elmwood getting prenatal care and learning what it means to be a teen mom.*

Emilia—*And what about her boyfriend, Scott? Is he going to Elmwood, too?*

Diego—*If he wants to—it's coed. Though, I'd be surprised if he does go there. I haven't discussed this with him. Only Jasmine and her parents have requested our guidance.*

Michael—*Are we making a hasty decision here? We might want to take a closer look at this. The interracial aspects of their relationship could have some backlash if we are not sensitive to these realities.*

Diego—*I don't see race or popularity as the issue here. I am concentrating on our responsibility to help this student. As much as I would like to see Jasmine continue here, her choices changed all that. I'm not trying to be insensitive, just realistic.*

Michael—*Can I suggest we back up here a moment and broaden the discussion? I have a couple of concerns. How did we lose sight of our agreement to meet monthly as a team to arrive at a consensus about these issues? Perhaps you reacted a bit hastily Diego by meeting with Jasmine and her parents without some input from us.*

Diego—*Maybe so, but the parents came to campus and I tried to deal with it. You know how busy it gets.*

Michael—*That happens, though I'd prefer that we strategize about this a bit more. The other concern is about our policy of sending pregnant teens to the alternative school. Is it in their best academic interest? Or, is this another policy that creates barriers rather than pathways to success? I'm concerned about the inequity that is about to happen to one more of our female students of color because of this policy?*

Diego—*Inequity? What do you mean?*

Michael—*Our counseling team looked at the data on transfers to Elmwood's pregnant minor program in the past four years, and the numbers keep rising. The policy limits the academic opportunities for these students. Even if the students return the next year, as you suggest, Diego, they have missed a semester or a year of AP classes while they are away, and that affects their GPA and their competitive edge in applying for colleges or career tech.*

Diego—*How can I make it all fair and just? I think we should look at the fact that our district provides a very good support system to these teen parents.*

Emilia—*Yes, they do, Diego; it helps a lot of kids. I'm just concerned that we not lump Jasmine in with the other females who got pregnant. Jasmine really has potential. In fact, I can't believe what I just said! All of the students who go to Elmwood are denied Pine Hills' rigorous curriculum, whether we recognize their potential or not!*

Michael—*Precisely, Emilia. Our school data shows that 42 females and 2 males from our school transferred to Elmwood for the pregnant minor program in these past four years. This is happening to a disproportionate number of our girls, and the majority of them are students of color.*

Diego—*Okay, what would you have us do?*

Michael—*I'd like us to hash these things out together as a team. Get our differences out here on the table and then take the bold step of developing and implementing some new policies. What if we coordinated services right here on campus after school or offered the services of the pregnant minor programs on Saturday so students can stay in their home school for academics and then attend extended hours learning about parenthood? What might be some ways for us to coordinate our resources in service of pregnant teens?*

Emilia—*Michael, you do have me thinking here. Why don't we offer AP classes at Elmwood? What about all those students suspended or expelled from our school and sent there?*

Michael—*Good question. That's another issue to explore.*

Diego—*I hear what you are saying. Quite honestly I did not know how many students we referred. You are bringing up some good points.*

Michael—*We understand your busy schedule. Our counseling team can assist. We are looking at the data, and finding many policies that don't serve all of our students equitably.*

Diego—*I appreciate your diligence, Michael, and your input, Emilia. I'd like to hear more. Bouncing these ideas off each other does help me to consider other ways of meeting our students' needs.*

Going Deeper

As you think about your school, in what ways do you believe you and your school provide equitable access and inclusivity to the broad, diverse range your students? In what ways do you believe more needs to be done? What evidence do you have to support either notion? Please use the space below to record your thinking. How might your thoughts be useful to school leaders?

_____

_____

_____

_____

_____

_____

9

Institutionalizing Cultural Knowledge Through Assessment and Use of Data

Educational practice, whether it be democratic or authoritarian, is always directive.

—Paulo Freire (1989, p. 79)

Getting Centered

Your school is a collection of cultures. The adults at the school represent numerous cultures. Your students and their families represent various cultures, even when they appear to be homogeneous. When thinking of the term *culture*, most likely you think of race, ethnicity, gender, faith, socioeconomics, sexual orientation, and/or ableness. In reflecting on your school, what other cultural groupings come to mind?

Take a moment and think about any one or more of these student groups in terms of their academic performance. Which ones are considered high performing? Which are considered low performing?

When thinking of access and achievement data, about which of the groups are data available to you and your colleagues? To guide and deepen your reflection and dialogue with colleagues, we pose two questions for your consideration:

- Of students who are high achieving, how familiar are you with their cultures?
- Of students who are low achieving, how familiar are you with their cultures?
- Use the space below to record your most honest, direct responses to the last two questions.

_____

_____

_____

_____

Most of us tend to be more familiar with the cultures of high-achieving students than we are with the cultures of low-achieving students. This may be because, in large part, we traveled a similar path to get to where we are today. We performed well, if not very well; caring educators supported us through most of our educational experiences; and, we learned how to navigate the expectations for being successful in school. Conversely, most of us have had limited, direct experience with students from cultural groups that have been historically marginalized.

From the time we were high school students, most likely we have been aware of low-achieving students' existence, and now, in our roles as educators, too often we learn that we do not know as much about them as we do higher achieving students. It is this disconnect that makes the essential element of _institutionalizing cultural knowledge_ fundamental to our and our schools' continuous learning. Paired with assessment and use of data, institutionalizing cultural knowledge becomes a powerful platform to guide our schools and us when we become leverage points for change in closing access and achievement gaps.

Institutionalizing Cultural Knowledge Through Assessment and Use of Data

A veritable gift of the accountability movement of the past decade has been the disaggregation of data. Having access and achievement data provide the opportunity to discuss culture in ways not imagined just a few years ago. Use of assessment data provides an entrée into learning about culture as a means to knowing the cultural context of our students and their communities in substantive ways. Having guided discussions about students' cultures part of educators' normal, everyday professional conversations can lead to interactions with parents/ guardians, community organizations, and local businesses that foster support systems for student achievement.

As with the other essential elements, *institutionalizing cultural knowledge* requires teachers, administrators, and counselors to engage in action and new behaviors grounded in the guiding principles. Table 9.1 portrays the role and function of counselors with regard to institutionalizing cultural knowledge, assessment, and use of data. Not only are functions in active voice, they are active in educator behavior and school practices.

Table 9.1   Institutionalizing Cultural Knowledge Through Assessment and Use of Data

Essential Element of Cultural Competence	TSCI 21st Century Counselor Role
Institutionalizing Cultural Knowledge	• Focuses school on academic success being primary • Promotes academic achievement • Focuses on whole-school and systemic issues

Institutionalizing Cultural Knowledge

Institutionalizing is a very powerful term. To institutionalize something is to make it usual. In the case of Cultural Proficiency, culture and learning about culture become part of the *usual* processes of school. To acknowledge, learn about, and use cultural knowledge are fundamental to the organizational culture of the school. As indicated in Table 9.1, the presence and availability of disaggregated data in our schools presents us with a tool to deepen our cultural knowledge in service of our students and their communities.

School leaders model and use collaborative and inclusive decision-making processes focused on a vision of closing access and achievement gaps for students. Data are used as vehicles for examining current educational practices, for assessing student progress, and for selecting inclusive practices that honor and support students' cultures as assets to their learning. In using data these ways, the school functions as a learning community committed to its own learning.

TSCI 21st Century Counselor Assessment and Use of Data

School counselor roles are pivotal to school leadership teams because of their access to data. Counselor skills in analyzing and interpreting data, and their skills in working with educator colleagues to ask questions of educators and school practices, can connect educator practice with student access and achievement. The most visible data available to schools are data that reflect student achievement, whether measured through standards-based assessments or nationally normed assessments. The skilled counselor understands the value and the limitation of each of these assessments and guides, and supports school administrators and teachers to ask questions that probe historical disparities, uncover current disproportionality, and speculate about *what if*. It is through these types of analyses that educators and their schools align their stated value for diversity, inclusivity, and access.

Institutionalizing Cultural Knowledge Through Assessment and Use of Data

At the beginning of this chapter, we made the case that often we know more about the cultures of high-performing students than we do about the culture of low-performing students. However, as a learning community, we have the capacity to learn about the cultures and lives of lower performing students as a means to developing a mutual interest in their success. Although there may be many avenues to our learning, most certainly, the presence of data is one important path readily available to us. In addition, and throughout this book, we emphasize the importance and value of personal reflection and dialogue with colleagues and community members. Following are questions adapted from Lindsey, Jungwirth, Pahl, and Lindsey (2009) to guide you and your colleagues as we all continue our journey as thoughtful and effective educators.

My Inside-Out Learning Process

- In what ways do I learn about our students' cultural communities, with particular emphasis on groups consistently identified as underachieving?

- In what ways do I develop and use assessment processes and data to benchmark student success indicators?
- To keep myself informed, I have been reading . . .
- I engage in inquiry to inform my thinking and actions for . . .

Reflections

Consider for a moment what you know about the cultures of some of the students in your school as well as those you may not know as well. Review the questions above and use the space below to record your thinking.

_____

_____

_____

_____

Facilitating My School's Inside-Out Learning Process About School Culture

- In what ways do I facilitate our school's learning about our students' cultural communities, with particular emphasis on groups consistently identified as underachieving?
- In what ways do I use assessment and data collection processes to inform a continuous improvement inquiry model focused on clearly stated access and achievement goals?
- In what ways do I use learning community modes, such as book studies, to facilitate faculty dialogue about culture?

Reflections

Use the space below to record the processes you use to address the questions above. Then, list some processes you will want to consider using with your colleagues.

_____

_____

_____

_____

Facilitating My School's Inside-Out Learning Process About the Community We Serve

- In what ways does our school engage with members of the community to learn of their aspirations for their children?
- In what ways does our school learn about the neighborhoods in which our students live?
- In what ways does our school engage parents/guardians as partners in the education of their children?

Reflections

In what ways do you engage learning about your community? In addition, how do you support and involve your educator colleagues learning about the community you serve?

_____

_____

_____

_____

Using the Rubric

Institutionalizing Cultural Knowledge Through Assessment and Use of Data

The rubric from Chapter 4 is designed to guide your inside-out approach to your and your school's learning. The focal point in this chapter is the fifth row of the rubric, the essential element *institutionalizing cultural knowledge* informed by assessment and use of data. Consider these steps to guide reading the rubric:

- Turn to Chapter 4, Table 4.1, Counselor Collaboration Rubric: Misuse to Use. Read the fifth row of the rubric, institutionalizing cultural knowledge. The changing tone of the rubric is striking as you read from Cultural Destructiveness to Cultural Proficiency.
- Table 9.2 presents the Institutionalizing Cultural Knowledge row of the rubric from Chapter 4. Please keep these in mind as you read:
  - Table 9.2 is limited to the positive side of the rubric. Of course, negative practices and voices to the left side of the

continuum are ever-present, but for our purposes, we focus to the right side of the rubric where illustration for responding to comments/practices represented as Cultural Destructiveness, Cultural Incapacity, or Cultural Blindness. Table 9.2 is designed movement from expressions and implied actions of others with statements such as *If their cultures had been important, I would have learned about them in school*, or *Diversity is just code for reverse racism and bigotry*, or *It isn't about race, really it is socioeconomic and lack of effort*. It is our belief that not knowing how to respond to such statements is important to recognize and acknowledge and to view the rubric as a lens for moving your internal thoughts to productive actions for you, your school, and the students in your school.

Please be aware that comments/practices on the left side of the rubric may come from you and not always from others. Being attentive to comments/practices located at any point of the rubric prepares you to use illustrations on the right side of the rubric as the basis for comments/practices for you and your colleagues. The rubric may be an important resource in the inside-out process of change for you and your school.

o The mantras' *active voice* and *intentionality* are characteristic of the culturally competent/proficient educator. As you read the passages for Cultural Precompetence, Cultural Competence, and Cultural Proficiency, continue to pay attention to adjectives and verbs and note both active voice and intentionality. The inside-out process for individuals and organizations leads to intentional change for every grade level and department in your school.

Pine View Middle School on Faith and Heterosexism

Pine View Middle School is rapidly becoming a model in the district for their commitment to culturally proficient practices. The leadership and counseling team enthusiastically embraces the opportunity to transform their school-counseling program, and they are thrilled to be included as equal participants in grade-level and leadership meetings. The decision to focus on whole-school reform has served them well in building a safe and supportive school climate. This focus is a welcome change for the school and for the district, given

Table 9.2 Institutionalizing Cultural Knowledge—New Role of 21st Century School Counselor

Five Essential Elements Informed by ASCA Domains • Academic • Career • Personal/Social Success	Cultural Precompetence	Cultural Competence— Informed by TSCI	Cultural Proficiency
Institutionalizing Cultural Knowledge— the extent to which cultural knowledge is evident in counselor and fellow educator behavior and in school practices.	School personnel beginning to regard evolving role of school counselor to include assessor of schoolwide student needs and not limited to provider of direct services. Counselor being included as collaborative member of leadership for instructional improvement with particular focus on achievement gap. Counselor serving as liaison between school and community/professional resources for determining culturally appropriate student support services.	Counselors and fellow educators structure opportunities for sharing expertise among school personnel. Counselors in conversation with all school personnel to provide updates on campus issues with structured time to brainstorm and set strategic plans to address areas of concern—data that highlight cultural/demographic discrepancies that have impeded school responses to achievement gaps. *Counselor role is:* • Achievement promoter. • To maintain focus on whole-school and system issues. • To keep primary focus of school on academic success.	Educators and school community view role of school counselor to be lead advocate for use of data to inform school of on-going successes and areas of continuous improvement as major components of systemic approach in serving the needs of a diverse student and community constituency.

that just three years ago they were in the national spotlight for the on-campus shooting of a gay student.

Three members of the leadership team are meeting today: Stacie, the assistant principal; Flora, the head school counselor; and Ed, the eighth-grade history; science teacher and afterschool coach. They are reviewing and discussing data gathered from a schoolwide needs assessment survey completed last year.[1] Let's join them as they consider how these data help them identify school issues and make plans to enhance academic achievement. Take particular note of the manner in which Stacie, Flora, and Ed *stay in the fire* when talking about topics that might become divisive, such as faith and sexual orientation.

> **Stacie**—*Well, did you see the achievement scores posted in the paper this morning?*
>
> **Ed**—*I didn't even look this time. I guess I'm a little hesitant to read about us again in the paper.*
>
> **Flora**—*I sure did. You might want to take a look at them tonight, Ed; I think it will be a real boost. We are out of program improvement now, and our achievement continues to climb for all of our students.*
>
> **Stacie**—*Yes! It's an exciting day! I just wanted to take a moment to acknowledge our success.*
>
> **Flora**—*Thank you, Stacie. Our schoolwide surveys these past three years have certainly helped our team in assessing student needs and program planning.*
>
> **Stacie**—*That part I understand, but how has this assessment work contributed to our students' academic achievement?*
>
> **Flora**—*The data show a steady decrease in suspensions and student attendance is up. More of our students are attending afterschool tutoring, and our parents are volunteering more time in the classrooms. Teacher morale is up. Wouldn't you say all of this is connected with our academic success?*
>
> **Ed**—*I would agree. I have sure learned a lot from our staff development. I remember wondering how could the new social-emotional curriculum embedded daily in the classroom increase our teaching time and reduce behavioral issues? I was a bit skeptical, questioning how my students would respond to the mindfulness activities facilitated by the counseling team and interns.*
>
> **Stacie**—*I wondered, too; that's why I visited the classrooms so often. I spent a few nights questioning what kind of banter and jokes are we going to get when asking our students to identify and define what GLBTQI means?*

---

[1]The Pine View Middle School Needs Assessment Survey is Resource B located in the Resource section of this book.

Ed—*Yeah, I wondered how I would become more comfortable discussing these hot-topic areas? As a teacher I signed up to teach the curriculum, never dreaming that these personal/social issues would come with the territory.*

Flora—*Looks like we really are making progress in teaching the whole student. I felt a shift happening within myself and with one another as colleagues last year at the cultural proficiency retreat. Remember how discussing the healthy practices on the continuum helped us with understanding of how to identify and respond to hetero-sexism, especially after the shooting on campus?*

Ed—*Oh yeah—boy did I learn things about myself. Here I thought I was so open, and a great advocate for the kids who were being taunted! Then I had to face the question how did my getting in a student's face about their antics contribute to the problems we were facing?*

Stacie—*I know what you mean. These self-reflective questions really have helped us define what more we can do to help our students and us. I'm really proud of our team here; we've really stepped up to the plate. How have our new ways of communicating and reflecting on our own values impacted the climate in the classrooms and on the playground?*

Flora—*The conversations are sure more positive, particularly in the staff lounge. I really do believe our discussion early in the year about our core values and relating them to the Guiding Principles of Cultural Proficiency has caused all of us to think more deeply about how we know our students and their cultures. Which brings us to the next steps in our five-year plan. Are we looking at some of the data now?*

Stacie—*Yeah, Flora—what have you counselors found from the latest survey?*

Flora—*A number of things. Four major issues surfaced. First, 72% of our faculty and staff think that the Newcomers group should continue. The other 28% feel that new students should just go to their classes the first day and find their own friends. Some teachers don't like student mentors being called out of class to meet and show a new student around. They think it is disruptive.*

Stacie—*Well 72% is a favorable response. Do we know if any of the student mentors are getting lower grades because of missing class? Could that be what concerns the teachers?*

Flora—*We are looking into this in more depth—a preliminary review does not show any change in their academics. So, I'm wondering, what more might we discuss together so that everyone understands the importance of helping new students make meaningful connections the moment they come to our school? What might be some dialogue topics on meaningful participation, belonging, and school safety that we might present?*

Stacie—*Let's reflect on it while we hear the other information you gathered.*

Flora—*Sure. Second major issue concerns our new faith-based clubs and our gay-straight alliance club. We are at about 60% of the teachers in favor and 40% who want them disbanded.*

Ed—*Any sense of what the objections are about?*

Flora—*They vary—many teachers questioned, "Isn't it inappropriate to have clubs that divide students in groups, celebrating their differences rather than focusing on their similarities?" Others only want clubs that support academic achievement, such as the math club, or the science club.*

Ed—*So, some don't get the connection between a sense of belonging at our school and academic success?*

Flora—*Not yet, but that takes time. So, let's think about this question: What more can we do to connect the dots for all of us?*

Stacie—*Seems to me that 60% is a good showing in support of the changes we have made. What about scheduling another staff development day to learn more about the connection between safety, prosocial bonding, and academics?*

Ed—*Great idea. I could benefit from more understanding of this myself.*

Stacie—*Flora, would you and your counseling team work on that?*

Flora—*Sure will. The third issue from the survey is how we are handling curriculum revisions. Incorporating the new reading books that promote asset building is a problem for the majority of the teachers. Over 70% feel it is distracting. It's interesting, though, because nearly 65% of the students are really enjoying them.*

Ed—*That is interesting—what's the disconnect between the teachers and the students?*

Flora—*Some teachers questioned how do we add one more thing to our busy days? Others wondered, "How are these books related to the subject I teach?"*

Ed—*Wow—I'm experiencing just the opposite. I like that my students are gravitating toward the books. Finally we are giving them topics that relate to their lives.*

Stacie—*Are you seeing any patterns in their books of interest, Ed?*

Ed—*It varies. I was so glad that we had a story of the Muslim family relocating to the United States. Our new student from Iran chose this book for her oral presentation. Our class had a great discussion, and the kids learned a lot about the Islamic faith. Some of my students took books on sexual orientation, and one of them did a report on the impact of heterosexism in schools. Another student selected a book on homeless youth. It sure provides for rich discussions about history and culture.*

Flora—*Well, there may be some connections between the issues of the books and the final area identified in the survey. Nearly 38% of our teachers questioned our continual discussion about culture. They say they just want to teach their classes. They are pretty insistent that faith and sexual orientation are private matters and should not be the focus in our schools. On the positive side of this, nearly 82% agreed that these topics are okay between the counselor and the student.*

Ed—*What's positive about suggesting to keep these discussions behind closed doors?*

Stacie:—*Could it be that more of the teachers are at least acknowledging that our students need someone to talk to about these areas?*

Flora—*Or, could it be that they see the value of having a school counselor help the students? Is our credibility growing? We are partnering with teachers more now in providing resources and support groups to enhance student study skills. Our pre- and posttests are a hit with the teachers. They are asking for more consultation and support.*

Stacie—*Great. Let's take time to study these results and reflect on what they mean to us. These assessments keep us connected with everyone and give some solid evidence of what we need to do next. Look over the data and consider, what might be some best next steps to take? What ways can we further develop an understanding and comfort with our staff and teachers about culture? In what ways might students express their impressions about our new curriculum? I'll put this on the agenda for our meeting next week.*

Going Deeper

How do you know what you don't know? This question is an indicator of the person who is moving from precompetence to competence and onto proficiency. Think about what you do know about the culture of your school, the cultures of the students, and the cultures within the community. What do you want to learn? How will you go about learning? In what ways will you lead your school in this learning?

_____

_____

_____

_____

_____

_____

PART III

Next Steps

10

Sustaining Culturally Proficient Counseling

Developing a Personal Action Plan

Sense of Urgency and Intentionality

Throughout this book, we have endeavored to paint a picture of urgency paired with hope. For many of our students, the situation is dire, and there are many variables beyond our control, which makes it ever more important to have direct, intentional impact over the time students are in our schools and classrooms. You have been introduced to the phrase "leverage point for change," and it has been applied to the role of school counselor actively involved with school leadership teams committed to narrowing and closing achievement gaps. The phrase "leverage point for change" also refers to the Counselor Collaboration Rubric: Misuse to Use presented in Chapter 4 and discussed in depth in Chapters 5–9. *These twin foci are intentional and urgent.*

Assume for a moment that the students in our schools not meeting academic standards needed to be successful in modern society were your children or grandchildren. Do you feel the urgency now? Next, focus on the role of school counselor by examining the contrasting roles of school counselor in Table 10.1. Which role description of

Table 10.1   Contrasting Roles of School Counselor

Traditional Role	21st Century Role
• Solitary • Protector of environment • Focus on scheduling and career advising • Unaware of student assets • Periphery of faculty and administrator discussions on student achievement • Unaware of community served by school	• Team member • Protector of students • Focus on academic achievement • Well aware of student assets • Central to leadership team discussion of student achievement and provider of data • Well aware of community, its challenges, and assets

school counselor do you want for your child or grandchild? Do you sense the intentionality of this book?

Of course, we expect you to opt for the 21st Century Role described in the right side column. You selected this book and have read this far because of an interest in improving your professional skills as a counselor or as an educator wanting to leverage the knowledge and skills of your school counselor on closing achievement gaps. Our approach, as you know, is described as an inside-out process. We wish you well as you continue your journey for you and your school. The school leadership team, with school counselors as integral members, is poised to sustain culturally proficient counseling initiatives.

The Inside-Out Process Is for You, Your School, and Your Community

The intent of this chapter is for you to develop a personal plan for yourself as a school counselor or for working with your school counselor. To this point you have learned about the evolving role of school counselors as members of school leadership teams, using professional standards to support the new role of school counselor, and using cultural proficiency as a lens to guide your work. You have had the opportunity to do the following:

- To reflect on your inside-out process for learning about your own culture, the culture of your school, and the culture of the community you serve;

- To reflect on your thinking and your practice; and,
- To read and study vignettes from the Maple View School District.

In this chapter, you are encouraged to summarize your learning and to design how you want to function as a member of a culturally proficient leadership team committed to access and equity for all students in your school. To prompt your thinking, tables from Chapters 5–9 have been replicated in this chapter.

Chapter 5—Assessing Cultural Knowledge Through Leadership

Table 10.2 is a reproduction of Table 5.1, Assessing Cultural Knowledge Through Leadership, and is brought forth in this chapter to serve as an anchor for your learning. The table aligns the essential element, Assessing Cultural Knowledge, with three functions of The Education Trust's 21st Century Counselor Role. To summarize your learning about the essential element and its relationship to the role of school counselor, you are guided through a three-step review and summary process as the initial step in designing your action plan.

Table 10.2   Assessing Cultural Knowledge Through Leadership

Essential Element of Cultural Competence	TSCI 21st Century Counselor Role
Assessing Cultural Knowledge	• Leader as planner and program developer • Leader for involvement with all stakeholders • Leader for academic focus on strengths

Step 1—Inside-Out Process. Take a few moments and browse through Chapter 5, paying particular attention to your reflective responses to the three inside-out learning processes. Review your entries and synthesize two reflections that represent the inside-out process relative to you, your school, and/or the community your school serves. Summarize your learning in the space below.

_____

_____

_____

_____

_____

_____

Step 2—Vignette. This time browse through the Chapter 5 vignette and summarize one or two key ideas you glean from reading the vignette again. Use the space below to summarize those key ideas.

_____

_____

_____

_____

_____

_____

Step 3—Getting Centered and Going Deeper. Read your reflections to the Chapter 5 opening and closing activities, paying particular attention to your reactions and your observations of self and others. Use the space below to summarize key learning and insights.

_____

_____

_____

_____

_____

_____

Chapter 6—Valuing Diversity Through Advocacy

Table 10.3 is a duplicate of Table 6.1, Valuing Diversity Through Advocacy, and is here as a reminder for your learning. The table aligns the essential element, Valuing Diversity, with three functions of The Education Trust's 21st Century Counselor Role. This time you are invited to return to Chapter 6 to summarize your learning about the essential element and its relationship to the role of school counselor, through the three-step review and summary process as the next step in developing your action plan.

Table 10.3   Valuing Diversity Through Advocacy

Essential Element of Cultural Competence	TSCI 21st Century Counselor Role
Valuing Diversity	• Advocate as an agent for change and equity • Advocate as a champion for all students • Advocate for inclusion of all

Step 1—Inside-Out Process. Return to Chapter 6, paying particular attention to your reflective responses to the three inside-out learning processes. Reread your recordings, and synthesize two reflections that represent your inside-out process relative to you, your school, and/or the community your school serves. The space below is provided for you to summarize your learning.

_____

_____

_____

_____

_____

_____

Step 2—Vignette. Browse through the Chapter 6 vignette and summarize one or two key ideas you take from the vignette. Use the space below to summarize those key ideas.

_____

_____

_____

_____

_____

_____

Step 3—Getting Centered and Going Deeper. Read your reflections to the Chapter 6 opening and closing activities. As you read, take note of any feelings that may surface for you and your observations of self and others. The space below is to summarize key learning and insights.

_____

_____

_____

_____

_____

_____

Chapter 7—Managing the Dynamics of Difference Through Teaming and Collaboration

Table 10.4 is a copy of Table 7.1, Managing the Dynamics of Difference Through Teaming and Collaboration, and serves as a reminder for your learning. The table aligns the essential element, Managing the Dynamics of Difference, with three functions of The Education Trust's 21st Century Counselor Role. By continuing this three-step review and summary process, you will progress in the development of a personal action plan.

Table 10.4   Managing the Dynamics of Difference Through Teaming and Collaboration

Essential Element of Cultural Competence	TSCI 21st Century Counselor Role
Managing Dynamics of Difference	• Broker of school-community resources • Data user for change agenda • Team leader accountable for student success

Step 1—Inside-Out Process. Revisit Chapter 7, focusing attention to your reflective responses to the three inside-out learning processes. Review your entries and synthesize two reflections that represent your inside-out process relative to you, your school, and/or the community your school serves. Summarize your learning in the space below.

_____

_____

_____

_____

_____

_____

Step 2—Vignette. Now, take a few moments and browse through the Chapter 7 vignette and summarize one or two key ideas that emerge from reading the vignette again. Use the space below to summarize those key ideas.

_____

_____

_____

_____

_____

_____

Step 3—Getting Centered and Going Deeper. Your reflections to the opening and closing activities may evoke certain reactions and observations about yourself and others. Use the space below to summarize reactions, learning, and insights.

_____

_____

_____

_____

_____

_____

Chapter 8—Adapting to Diversity Through Counseling and Coordination

Table 10.5 is the same as Table 8.1, Adapting to Diversity Through Counseling and Coordination, here as a reminder for your learning. The table aligns the essential element, Adapting to Diversity, with three functions of The Education Trust's 21st Century Counselor Role. You are now very familiar with the three-step review and summary process provided to support you in designing your action plan.

Table 10.5   Adapting to Diversity Through Counseling and Coordination

Essential Element of Cultural Competence	TSCI 21st Century Counselor Role
Adapting to Diversity	• Coordinates educational team • Coordinates teaming and collaboration • Coordinates a focused mission with responsibilities

Step 1—Inside-Out Process. Take another look at Chapter 8 rereading your reflective responses to the three inside-out learning processes. Construct two reflections prompted in this reread that represent the inside-out process relative to you, your school, and/or the community your school serves. Use the space below to summarize your thinking.

_____

_____

_____

_____

_____

Step 2—Vignette. Summarize one or two key ideas you gather from reading the Chapter 8 vignette again. Use the space below to summarize those key ideas.

_____

_____

_____

_____

_____

Step 3—Getting Centered and Going Deeper. Be mindful of your reactions and observations of self and others as you reread your reflections to the Chapter 8 opening and closing activities. The space below is for you to summarize key learning and insights.

_____

_____

_____

_____

_____

_____

Chapter 9—Institutionalizing Cultural Knowledge Through Assessment and Use of Data

Table 10.6 is a reproduction of Table 9.1, Institutionalizing Cultural Knowledge Through Assessment and Use of Data. Table 9.1 is placed here for your quick review and as a reminder for your learning. The table aligns the essential element, Institutionalizing Cultural Knowledge, with three functions of The Education Trust's 21st Century Counselor Role. This is the final three-step review activity to summarize learning about an essential element and its relationship to the role of school counselor to be used in designing your action plan.

Table 10.6   Institutionalizing Cultural Knowledge Through Assessment and Use of Data

Essential Element of Cultural Competence	TSCI 21st Century Counselor Role
Institutionalizing Cultural Knowledge	• Focuses school on academic success being primary • Promotes academic achievement • Focuses on whole-school and systemic issues

Step 1—Inside-Out Process. Look through Chapter 9, attending to your reflective responses to the three inside-out learning processes. Review your entries, and synthesize two reflections that represent your inside-out process relative to you, your school, and/or the community your school serves. Summarize your learning in the space below.

_____

_____

_____

_____

_____

_____

Step 2—Vignette. Take a few moments to peruse through the Chapter 9 vignette, and then summarize one or two key ideas you glean from reading the vignette again. The space below is for you to summarize those key ideas.

_____

_____

_____

_____

_____

_____

Step 3—Getting Centered and Going Deeper. Reread your reflections to Chapter 9's opening and closing activities. What do you notice about your reactions and your observations of self and others? Use the space below to summarize key learning and insights.

_____

_____

_____

_____

_____

_____

From Words to Action

Seven Steps for Providing Equity Using Chapters 5–9

1. Use the space below to summarize your reactions/feelings to the reading and reflective activities. Your summary may be key words, or you may choose a longer, expository approach.

_____

_____

_____

_____

_____

_____

2. As you read and analyze what you have written, what insights do you have about yourself as an educator working in a diverse setting to provide access and equitable opportunity to students?

_____

_____

_____

_____

_____

_____

3. In what ways does the inside-out approach of Cultural Proficiency contribute to learning about yourself?

_____

_____

_____

_____

_____

_____

4. In what ways does the inside-out approach contribute to learning about the culture of your school?

_____

_____

_____

_____

_____

_____

5. In what ways does the inside-out approach contribute to learning about the community your school serves?

_____

_____

_____

_____

_____

6. Now that you know what you know, what three commitments are you willing to make to be an advocate for equity in your school?

_____

_____

_____

_____

_____

7. In what ways will you, as a counselor, support equity in your school? If you are not a counselor, in what ways will you work with your counselor to support equity in your school? What three bold steps will you be taking within the next three to six months to demonstrate your commitments?

_____

_____

_____

_____

_____

_____

The next steps to sustaining a culturally proficient educational environment for your students are up to you and your colleagues. For our preK–12 schools to serve our diverse society in ways that are equitable and will meet the 21st century needs of a democracy, call upon the will and skill of all educators. In this book, we have focused on the school counselor and educators who work with counselors to address issues of equity and inequity rooted in historical and endemic forces. These forces can be confronted and circumvented. Within each of us and within our moral commitment lie voices of hope and desire. Now, let's move toward action in our schools and communities.

Resource D

Resource D, Online Resources for Educator Use, located in the back of the book, is composed of annotated references for your and your colleagues' use. We commend them for your continued professional development and look forward to your sharing with us references that you value.

Diana—dstephen@callutheran.edu
Randy—randallblindsey@gmail.com

Resources

Resource A

Maple View School District Vignette Storyboard

Essential Element Informed by TSCI Scope of Practice	Essential Element Informed by TSCI Scope of Practice	Essential Element Informed by TSCI Scope of Practice	Essential Element Informed by TSCI Scope of Practice	Essential Element Informed by TSCI Scope of Practice
Assessing cultural knowledge through leadership	Valuing diversity through advocacy	Managing the dynamics of difference through teaming and collaboration	Adapting to diversity through counseling & coordination	Institutionalizing cultural knowledge through assessment & use of data
Cultural Issue	**Cultural Issue**	**Cultural Issue**	**Cultural Issue**	**Cultural Issue**
• Ethnocentrism • English learning	• Sexism • Ableism	• Ethnocentrism • English learning • Classism	• Sexism • Racism	• Heterosexism • Issues of faith/spiritualism or absence thereof
TSCI 21st Century role is:	**TSCI 21st Century role is:**	**TSCI 21st Century role is:**	**TSCI 21st Century role is:**	**TSCI 21st Century role is:**
• Leader, planner, program developer • Involved with all stakeholders • To maintain academic focus on strengths	• Agent for change & equity • Champion for all students • Advocate for inclusion of all	• Broker of school-community resources • Data user for change agenda • To be accountable for student success	• Integral educational team member • To foster teaming & collaboration • Focused on mission & responsibilities	• Academic achievement promoter • To maintain focus on whole-school & system issues • To keep primary focus of school on academic success

Scenario: Maple View Elementary	Scenario: Pine View Middle School	Scenario: Pine Hills High School	Scenario: Pine Hills High School	Scenario: Pine View Middle School
• Gracie – Principal • Gabriella – Counselor • Sandy – Teacher	• Stacie – Assistant Principal • Flora – Counselor • Ed – Teacher	• Diego – Principal • Michael – Counselor • Emilia – Teacher	• Diego – Principal • Michael – Counselor • Emilia – Teacher	• Stacie – Assistant Principal • Flora – Counselor • Ed – Teacher
Issue/Action Steps	**Issue/Action Steps**	**Issue/Action Steps**	**Issue/Action Steps**	**Issue/Action Steps**
• Assessment instrument to explore school climate and diversity; goal of creating safe school environment to counter bullying, violence, gang posturing. • Infusing social-emotional learning curriculum in all classes.	• Building culture of support and safety following on-campus shooting of gay student. • Exploring support for discussions of gender, race, and discrimination. • Healthy kids initiative to combat juvenile obesity.	• Ethnic disparity in access to advanced placement classes; gender and ethnic disparity in suspensions. • Identifying ethnocentric views, myths re: English language learners; conditions of poverty. • Collaborative approach to	• Inequitable policies/gender bias re: handling of pregnant minors. • Use of data in identifying and changing policies impeding student access to rigorous curriculum. • Identifying barriers, creating pathways to support via	• Whole-school reform three years following on-campus shooting of gay student. • Whole-child approach to teaching; dialogue re: sexual orientation, heterosexism, faith. • Embracing self-reflection, on

(Continued)

(Continued)

• Initiating cross-cultural learning/self-reflection re: ethnocentric views that impact student success, parental participation, and community engagement.	• Identifying personal and social impediments to academic success.	closing achievement gap; identifying policies that perpetuate inequity and lack of access to resources/opportunities for student achievement.	coordination of services, increasing access to resources.	values that enhance/impede student progress. • Integrating knowledge and respect for cultural differences as an asset in the school; modeling ways to embrace all students and create environments that supports rigorous academic achievement – faith-based clubs, and gay-straight alliance clubs.

Stephens, Diana L., & Lindsey, Randall B. (2011). *Culturally proficient collaboration: Use and misuse of school counselors.* Thousand Oaks, CA: Corwin. Permission for exclusive use by purchasers of this book.

Resource B

Pine View Middle School

Schoolwide Needs Assessment (Teacher Version)

Grade Level:	6th _____	7th _____	8th _____

Teacher support: Select the three most important areas of support from the counseling department that would be most beneficial in our collaborative effort to increase student engagement and academic achievement:

- ❏ Strategies for positive behavior support and classroom management
- ❏ Collaborative consultation with parents/guardians/foster-care providers
- ❏ In-service professional development on personal/social issues for middle-school students
- ❏ Mediating parent concerns
- ❏ Class observations/feedback on student engagement
- ❏ Cross-age tutoring
- ❏ Professional consultation one-on-one
- ❏ Periodic data reports (student achievement, attendance, discipline)
- ❏ Student interventions
- ❏ Classroom guidance lessons (see topics below)

Other:_____

Other:_____

Other:_____

Student support: Throughout the year, student needs vary. Please indicate on the list below which areas are most essential for counselor focus this year in supporting student engagement and academic achievement. Please number these from 1 to 10 (1 = most needed).

____	Test-taking strategies	____	Friendships/Relationships
____	Study skills	____	Decision-making/Choices
____	Note taking	____	Internet protocols
____	Organization/Time management	____	Bullying/Harassment
____	Stress management	____	Self-esteem
____	Social skills	____	School connectedness
____	Grief and loss	____	Other:
____	Anger management	____	Other:

There are multiple ways that counselors are available to support your work with students. Please indicate below by a checkmark your preferred delivery mode:

- ❏ Guidance lessons presented in small groups to select students (outside classroom)
- ❏ Guidance lessons presented to all students in the classroom
- ❏ Guidance lessons presented individually as interventions

Below are a list of activities, practices, and curricular enhancements implemented last year. Please indicate your assessment of the effectiveness of these areas in supporting student engagement and academic achievement.

Please circle the number below that best describes your assessment of these new areas.

1 = extremely effective	2 = effective	3 = marginally effective	4 = not effective

Newcomer's group	1	2	3	4
Faith-based club	1	2	3	4
Gay-Straight Alliance Club	1	2	3	4
Afterschool tutoring	1	2	3	4
Books for youth focused on cultural issues/diversity	1	2	3	4

Please indicate below what you believe to be the most effective practices in supporting student engagement and academic achievement.

_____

_____

_____

Please indicate below what you believe needs to be changed, because it is not effective in supporting student engagement and academic achievement.

_____

_____

_____

Please add any additional comments/questions/suggestions.

_____

_____

_____

Resource C

Cultural Proficiency Books' Matrix

How to Use Our Books

Book	Authors	Focus
Cultural Proficiency: *A Manual for School Leaders,* **3rd Ed., 2009**	Randall B. Lindsey Kikanza Nuri Robins Raymond D. Terrell	This book is an introduction to cultural proficiency. There is extended discussion of each of the tools and the historical framework for diversity work.
Culturally Proficient Instruction: *A Guide for People Who Teach,* **2nd Ed., 2002**	Kikanza Nuri Robins Randall B. Lindsey Delores B. Lindsey Raymond D. Terrell	This book focuses on the five essential elements and can be directed to anyone in an instructional role. This book can be used as a workbook for a study group.
The Culturally Proficient School: *An Implementation Guide for School Leaders,* **2005**	Randall B. Lindsey Laraine M. Roberts Franklin CampbellJones	This book guides the reader to examine her school as a cultural organization and to design and implement approaches to dialogue and inquiry.
Culturally Proficient Coaching: *Supporting Educators to Create Equitable Schools,* **2007**	Delores B. Lindsey Richard S. Martinez Randall B. Lindsey	This book aligns the essential elements with Costa and Garmston's Cognitive Coaching model. The book provides coaches, teachers, and administrators a personal guidebook with protocols and maps for conducting conversations that shift thinking in support of all students achieving at levels higher than ever before.

Book	Authors	Focus
Culturally Proficient Inquiry: *A Lens for Identifying and Examining Educational Gaps,* 2008	Randall B. Lindsey Stephanie M. Graham R. Chris Westphal, Jr. Cynthia L. Jew	This book uses protocols for gathering and analyzing student achievement and access data as well as rubrics for gathering and analyzing data about educator practices. A CD accompanies the book for easy downloading and use of the data protocols.
Culturally Proficient Leadership: *The Personal Journey Begins Within,* 2009	Raymond D. Terrell Randall B. Lindsey	This book guides the reader through the development of a cultural autobiography as a means to becoming an increasingly effective leader in our diverse society.
Culturally Proficient Learning Communities: *Confronting Inequity Through Collaborative Curiosity,* 2009	Delores B. Lindsey Linda D. Jungwirth Jarvis V.N.C. Pahl Randall B. Lindsey	This book provides readers a lens through which to examine the purpose, the intentions, and the progress of learning communities to which they belong or wish to develop. School and district leaders are provided protocols, activities, and rubrics to engage in actions focused on the intersection of race, ethnicity, gender, social class, sexual orientation and identity, faith, and ableness with the disparities in student achievement.
The Cultural Proficiency Journey: *Moving Beyond Ethical Barriers toward Profound School Change,* 2010	Franklin CampbellJones Brenda CampbellJones Randall B. Lindsey	This book explores cultural proficiency as an ethical construct. It makes transparent the connection between values, assumptions, and beliefs, and observable behavior, making change possible and sustainable.

(Continued)

(Continued)

Book	Authors	Focus
Culturally Proficient Education: *An Assets-Based Response to Conditions of Poverty,* 2010	Randall B. Lindsey Michelle S. Karns Keith Myatt	This book is designed for educators to learn how to identify and develop the strengths of students from low-income backgrounds.
Culturally Proficient Collaboration: *Use and Misuse of School Counselors,* **2011**	Diana L. Stephens Randall B. Lindsey	This book uses the lens of Cultural Proficiency to frame the American School Counselor Association national model and The Education Trust's Transforming School Counseling Initiative as means for addressing issues of access and equity in schools in collaborative school leadership teams.
Culturally Proficient Organizations: *A Conversation With Colleagues About the Practice of Cultural Proficiency* **(working title), 2011**	Kikanza J. Nuri Delores B. Lindsey	This book answers the question, "How do you do it?" It is directed to managers and organizational leaders who want to introduce cultural proficiency systemically.

Stephens, Diana L., & Lindsey, Randall B. (2011). *Culturally proficient collaboration: Use and misuse of school counselors.* Thousand Oaks, CA: Corwin. Permission for exclusive use by purchasers of this book.

Resource D

Online Resources for Educators

Websites

California Counselor Leadership Network (CCLN)

Los Angeles County Office of Education

www.lacoe.edu/ccla

CCLN provides technical assistance, publication and distribution of "Getting Ready" transition guides (www.schoolguides.org), coordination of the Support Personnel Accountability Report Card (SPARC; www.sparconline.net), and professional development to the K–adult school counseling community.

CESCal: Center for Excellence in School Counseling and Leadership

www.cescal.org

Provides training by national leaders in school counseling, online support for creating school counseling programs and consultation from state and national leaders in school counseling and administration with experience in implementing ASCA National Model school counseling programs.

The George Lucas Educational Foundation

www.edutopia.org

Through the Edutopia.org website, *Edutopia* magazine, and *Edutopia* video, we spread the word about ideal, interactive learning environments and enable others to adapt these successes locally. Edutopia.org contains a deep archive of continually updated best practices, from classroom tips to recommendations for district-wide change.

The Lesson One Foundation

www.lessonone.org

Schoolwide program that gives adults a proven plan to help children develop the life skills and internal discipline necessary to learn and thrive in today's society. Lesson One works with children, teachers, staff, parents, and guardians to create an environment where children learn to integrate skills from self-control to cooperation into their lives.

Los Angeles Museum of Tolerance

www.museumoftolerance.com

Visitors become witnesses to history and explore the dynamics of bigotry and discrimination that are still embedded in society today. Interactive exhibits, special events, and customized programs exist for youths and adults. Teacher resources are available.

National School Climate Center (NSCC) (formerly Center for Social and Emotional Education [CSEE])

www.schoolclimate.org

NSCC offers a variety of professional development programs and services to support K–12 schools, afterschool settings, educators, parent advocate groups and states to support sustained school climate improvement efforts.

New Directions

http://www.genesislight.com/scan21st/tell_us/

Interactive site to post own reaction to prompts and read other perspectives regarding 21st century school counselors.

Operation Respect

www.operationrespect.org

Free "Don't Laugh at Me" curriculum provided for educators. Designed to inspire students, along with their teachers and other educators, to transform their classrooms and schools into "Ridicule Free Zones."

Resiliency in Action

www.resiliency.com

Provides training and resources on develop resiliency in students and creating resilient schools. Books and pamphlets available for purchase, offers speakers for presentations, and links to further your research.

Search Institute

www.search-institute.org

Search Institute is an independent nonprofit organization whose mission is to provide leadership, knowledge, and resources to promote healthy children, youth, and communities. Provide tools, resources, and services to equip parents, educators, youth workers, policymakers, and other leaders to create a world where all young people are valued and thrive.

Teaching Tolerance: A Project of the Southern Poverty Law Center

www.teachingtolerance.org

Free educational materials to teachers and other school practitioners in the United States and abroad. Teaching Tolerance's Mix It Up program helps K–12 teachers develop inclusive school communities.

References

American School Counselor Association. (1998). *The national standards for school counseling programs.* Alexandria, VA: Author.

American School Counselor Association. (2003). *The ASCA national model: A framework for school counseling programs.* Alexandria, VA: Author.

American School Counselor Association. (2005). *The ASCA national model: A framework for school counseling programs* (2nd ed.). Alexandria, VA: Author.

Books, Sue. (2004). *Poverty and schooling in the U.S.: Context and consequences.* New York: Lawrence Erlbaum and Associates, Taylor & Francis Group.

Bowers, Judy L., & Hatch, Patricia A. (2003). *The ASCA national model: A framework for school counseling programs.* Alexandria, VA: American School Counselor Association.

Buenida, Edward, Ares, Nancy, Juarez, Brenda, & Peercy, Megan. (2004). The geographies of difference: The production of east side, west side, and central city school. *American Educational Research Journal, 41*(4), 833–863.

Campbell, Chari A., & Dahir, Carol A. (1997). *Sharing the vision: The national standards for school counseling programs.* Alexandria, VA: American School Counselor Association.

CampbellJones, Brenda. (2002). *Against the stream: White men who act in ways to eradicate racism and white privilege/entitlement in the United States of America.* Unpublished doctoral dissertation, Claremont Graduate University, California.

CCTC, California Commission on Teacher Credentialing. (2001, January). *Standards of quality and effectiveness for Pupil Personnel Services Credentials: School counseling, school psychology, school social work, child welfare and attendance.* Sacramento, CA: Author.

CCTC, California Commission on Teacher Credentialing. (2006, January). *Submission guidelines for documents prepared to standards by the Commission on Teacher Credentialing for programs of Pupil Personnel Services credential programs: School Counseling, School Psychology, School Social Work, Child Welfare and Attendance.* Sacramento, CA: Author. Retrieved from http://www.ctc.ca.gov/educator-prep/standards/pps-SubGuide.pdf

Chávez, César. (2010). *César Chávez quotes.* Retrieved from http://www.great-quotes.com/quotes/author/Cesar/Chavez

Cross, Terry L., Bazron, Barbara J., Dennis, Karl W., & Isaacs, Mareasa R. (1989). *Toward a culturally competent system of care: Vol. 1.* Washington, DC: Georgetown University Child Development Program, Child and Adolescent Service System Program.

Dahir, Carol A., & Stone, Carolyn B. (2003). Accountability: A M.E.A.S.U.R.E. of the impact school counselors have on student achievement. *Professional School Counseling, 6,* 214–221.

DeVoss, Joyce A., & Andrews, Minie F. (2006). *School counselors as educational leaders.* Boston, MA: Houghton Mifflin.

The Education Trust. (1997, February). *The national guidance and counseling reform program.* Washington, DC: Author.

The Education Trust. (1998). *Transforming school counseling initiative* [Brochure]. Washington, DC: Author.

The Education Trust. (n.d., a). *History of TSCI.* Retrieved from http://www .edtrust.org/node/139

The Education Trust. (n.d., b). *National Center for Transforming School Counseling (NCTSC).* Retrieved from http://www.edtrust.org/dc/tsc

The Education Trust. (n.d., c). *New vision for school counseling.* Retrieved from http://www.edtrust.org/dc/tsc/vision

Ellis, Thomas I. (1991). *Guidance—The heart of education: Three exemplary approaches* (Report No. 328829). Ann Arbor: School of Education, University of Michigan. (ERIC Document Reproduction Service No. 328829)

Elementary and Secondary Education Act (ESEA). (2001). No Child Left Behind Act of 2001, Pub. L. No. 107-110, 115 Stat. 1425. Retrieved from http://www2.ed.gov/policy/elsec/leg/esea02/index.html

Fitch, John A. (1936). *Counseling: A comprehensive profession* (3rd ed.). Upper Saddle River, NJ: Merrill.

Frankl, Victor E. (1984). *Man's search for meaning.* New York: Pocket Books.

Freire, Paulo. (1987). *Pedagogy of the oppressed.* New York: Continuum.

Freire, Paulo. (1989). *Pedagogy of hope: Reliving pedagogy of the oppressed.* New York: Continuum.

Gladding, Samuel T. (1996). *Counseling: A comprehensive profession* (3rd ed.). Upper Saddle River, NJ: Merrill.

Gysbers, Norman C. (2001). School guidance and counseling in the 21st century: Remember the past into the future. *Professional School Counseling, 5,* 96–105.

Gysbers, Norman C. (2002). Comprehensive school guidance programs in the future: Staying the course. In Clarence D. Johnson & Sharon K. Johnson (Eds. & Contributors), *Building stronger school counseling programs: Bringing futuristic approaches into the present* (pp. 145–154). Greensboro, NC: CAPS Publications.

Gysbers, Norman C. (2004). Comprehensive guidance and counseling programs: The evolution of accountability. *Professional School Counseling, 8*(1), 1–14.

Gysbers, Norman C., & Henderson, Patricia. (2000). *Developing and managing your school guidance program.* Alexandria, VA: American Counseling Association.

Gysbers, Norman C., & Henderson, Patricia. (2001). Comprehensive guidance and counseling programs: A rich history and a bright future. *ASCA Professional School Counseling, 4*(4), 246–256.

Gysbers, Norman C., & Moore, Earle J. (1981). *Improving guidance programs.* Englewood Cliffs, NJ: Prentice-Hall.

Gysbers, Norman C., & Moore, Earle J. (1974). *Career guidance, counseling and placement: Elements of an illustrative program guide.* Columbia: Career Guidance, Counseling and Placement Project, University of Missouri-Columbia.

Hatch, Patricia A. (2002). National standards for school counseling programs: A source of legitimacy or reform? Unpublished doctoral dissertation, University of California at Riverside.

Henderson, Patricia, & Gysbers, Norman C. (1998). *Leading and managing your school guidance program staff.* Alexandria, VA: American Counseling Association.

Hines, Peggy, & Robinson, Stephanie. (2006). A diverse past and even more diverse future. *Professional School Counseling, 43*(3), 33.

House, Reese, Martin, Patricia, & Ward, Colin C. (2002). Changing school counselor preparation: A critical need. In Clarence D. Johnson & Sharon K. Johnson (Eds. & Contributors), *Building stronger school counseling programs: Bringing futuristic approaches into the present* (pp. 185–208). Greensboro, NC: CAPS Publications.

Hughes, Debbie K., & James, Susan H. (2001). Using accountability data to protect a school counseling program: One counselor's experience. *Professional School Counseling, 4,* 306–309.

Johnson, Sharon K., & Johnson, Clarence D. (1991). The new guidance: A systems approach to pupil personnel programs. *California Association of Counseling and Development Journal, 11,* 5–14.

Johnson, Sharon K., & Johnson, Clarence D. (2003). Results-based guidance: A systems approach to student support programs. *Professional School Counseling, 6,* 180–184.

Lambie, Glenn W., & Williamson, Laurie L. (2004). The challenge to change guidance Counseling to professional school counseling: A historical proposition. *Professional School Counseling, 4,* 125–131.

Lee, Courtland C., & Workman, D. J. (1992). School counselors and research: Current status and future direction. *The School Counselor, 40,* 15–19.

Lindsey, Delores B., Jungwirth, Linda D., Pahl, Jarvis V. N. C., & Lindsey, Randall B. (2009). *Culturally proficient learning communities: Confronting inequities through collaborative curiosity.* Thousand Oaks, CA: Corwin.

Lindsey, Randall, B., Karns, Michelle S., & Myatt, Keith. (2010). *Culturally proficient education: An assets-based approach to conditions of poverty.* Thousand Oaks, CA: Corwin.

Lindsey, Randall B., Nuri Robins, Kikanza, & Terrell, Raymond. (2009). *Cultural proficiency: A manual for school leaders* (3rd ed.). Thousand Oaks, CA: Corwin.

Myers, George E. (1923). Critical review of present developments in vocational guidance with special references to future prospects. *The Vocational Guidance Magazine, 2,* 139–142.

Myrick, Robert D. (1997). *Developmental guidance and counseling: A practical approach* (3rd ed.). Minneapolis, MN: Educational Media.

Myrick, Robert D. (2003). Accountability: Counselors count. *Professional School Counseling, 6,* 174–179.

National Defense Education Act of 1958, Pub. L. No. 85-864, 70 Stat. 1580-1605 (1959).

Parsons, Frank. (1909). *Choosing a vocation.* Boston, MA: Houghton Mifflin.

Perie, Marianne, Moran, Rebecca, & Lutkus, Anthony D. (2005). *NAEP 2004 trends in academic progress three decades of student performance in reading and mathematics.* Washington, DC: U.S. Department of Education. Retrieved from http://nces.ed.gov/pubsearch/pubsinfo.asp?pubid=2005464

Race to the Top. (2009). *Promoting innovation, reform, and excellence in America's public schools.* Retrieved from http://www.whitehouse.gov/the-press-office/fact-sheet-race-top

Schmidt, John J. (2003). *Counseling in schools: Essential services and comprehensive programs.* Boston, MA: Pearson Education.

Sciarra, Daniel T. (2004). *School counseling: Foundations and contemporary issues.* Belmont, CA: Brooks/Cole-Thomson Learning.

Senge, Peter, Cambron-McCabe, Nelda, Lucas, Timothy, Smith, Bryan, Dutton, Janice, & Kleiner, Art. (2000). *Schools that learn: A fifth discipline fieldbook for educators, parents, and everyone who cares about education.* New York: Doubleday.

Singleton, Glenn E., & Linton, Curtis W. (2006). *Courageous conversations.* Thousand Oaks, CA: Corwin.

Stephens, Geralyn E. (1995). *A comparative analysis of findings: Smith-Hughes Act of 1917 and The School-to-Work Opportunities Act of 1994.* Retrieved from http://www.eric.ed.gov/ERICWebPortal/recordDetail?accno=ED389852

Stone, Carolyn B., & Dahir, Carol A. (2011). *School counselor accountability: A MEASURE of success* (3rd ed.). Upper Saddle River, NJ: Merrill/Prentice Hall.

Terrell, Raymond D., & Lindsey, Randall B. (2009). *Culturally proficient leadership: The personal journey begins within.* Thousand Oaks, CA: Corwin.

Tutu, Archbishop Desmond. (2010). *Heroes for a better world.* Retrieved from http://www.betterworldheroes.com/pages-t/tutu-quotes.htm

Uellendahl, Gail, Stephens, Diana L., Buono, Lisa, & Lewis, Rolla. (2009). Support Personnel Accountability Report Card (SPARC): A measure to support school counselor accountability efforts. *Journal of School Counseling, 7*(32). Retrieved from http://jsc.montana.edu/articles/v7n32.pdf

Williamson, Edmund G. (1939). *How to counsel students.* New York: McGraw-Hill.

Yell, Mitchell L., & Drasgow, Erik. (2005). *No Child Left Behind: A guide for professionals.* Kent, OH: Merrill Prentice Hall.

Zunker, Vernon G. (2002). *Career counseling: Applied concepts of life planning* (6th ed.). Pacific Grove, CA: Brooks/Cole.

Index

CORWIN
A SAGE Company

The Corwin logo—a raven striding across an open book—represents the union of courage and learning. Corwin is committed to improving education for all learners by publishing books and other professional development resources for those serving the field of PreK–12 education. By providing practical, hands-on materials, Corwin continues to carry out the promise of its motto: **"Helping Educators Do Their Work Better."**